GRAVEL RIDES
LAKE DISTRICT

GRAVEL RIDES
LAKE DISTRICT

15 gravel bike adventures in Cumbria

ANDREW BARLOW

Vertebrate Publishing, Sheffield
www.adventurebooks.com

GRAVEL RIDES
LAKE DISTRICT

---

15 gravel bike adventures in Cumbria

First published in 2024 by Vertebrate Publishing. Reprinted in 2024.

 Vertebrate Publishing
Omega Court, 352 Cemetery Road, Sheffield S11 8FT, United Kingdom.
www.adventurebooks.com

Copyright © 2024 Andrew Barlow and Vertebrate Publishing Ltd.

Andrew Barlow has asserted his rights under the Copyright, Designs and Patents Act 1988 to be identified as author of this work.

A CIP catalogue record for this book is available from the British Library.

ISBN 978-1-83981-184-5 (Paperback)
ISBN 978-1-83981-185-2 (Ebook)

All rights reserved. No part of this work covered by the copyright herein may be reproduced or used in any form or by any means – graphic, electronic, or mechanised, including photocopying, recording, taping, or information storage and retrieval systems – without the written permission of the publisher.

Front cover *On Askham Fell above Ullswater (route 06).*
Back cover *The start of the descent from Askham Fell to Howtown (route 06).*
Opposite *Descent on Askham Fell towards Howtown (route 06).*
Photography by **Andrew Barlow** unless otherwise credited.

 All maps reproduced by permission of Ordnance Survey on behalf of The Controller of His Majesty's Stationery Office. © Crown Copyright. AC0000809882.

Edited by Helen Parry, design and production by Jane Beagley.
www.adventurebooks.com

Printed and bound in Bulgaria by Pulsio.

Vertebrate Publishing is committed to printing on paper from sustainable sources.

Every effort has been made to achieve accuracy of the information in this guidebook. The authors, publishers and copyright owners can take no responsibility for: loss or injury (including fatal) to persons; loss or damage to property or equipment; trespass, irresponsible behaviour or any other mishap that may be suffered as a result of following the route descriptions or advice offered in this guidebook. The inclusion of a track or path as part of a route, or otherwise recommended, in this guidebook does not guarantee that the track or path will remain a right of way. If conflict with landowners arises we advise that you act politely and leave by the shortest route available. If the matter needs to be taken further then please take it up with the relevant authority.

PLEASE GIVE WAY TO HORSES AND PEDESTRIANS.

CONTENTS

Introduction ix
Acknowledgements x
How to use this book x
Rights of way xi
Bikepacking xii
The bike xiii
Recommended kit list xiv
General safety xv
In the event of an accident xvi
Rules of the (off) road xvi
Planning your ride xvii
Maps & symbols xvii

SECTION 1 – EASY ROUTES
01 ■ Force Crag Mine & the Coledale Valley – **17.4km** 3
02 ■ Blawith Common – **17.4km** 9
03 ■ Loughrigg loop – **18.1km** 15
04 ■ Ambleside, Hawkshead & Claife Heights – **26.6km** 21

SECTION 2 – STRAIGHTFORWARD ROUTES
05 ■ St John's in the Vale & Keswick Railway Path – **19.3km** . . . 29
06 ■ Askham Fell – **20.4km** 35
07 ■ Glenderaterra – **18.4km** 39
08 ■ Keswick & the Newlands Valley – **23.9km** 45
09 ■ Tilberthwaite & Langdale – **25.2km** 51
10 ■ Grizedale Forest – **38km** 57
11 ■ Staveley to shoreside – **48km** 63

SECTION 3 – CHALLENGING ROUTES
12 ■ Kentmere – **17km** 71
13 ■ The other Borrowdale – **31km** 77
14 ■ Skiddaw House & the Old Coach Road – **57.3km** 83
15 ■ Lakeland 270 – **270km** 91

Appendix 98

Download the Gravel Rides
Lake District GPX files from
www.adventurebooks.com/GRLD-GPX

Route grades
■ Easy   ■ Straightforward
■ Challenging

GRAVEL RIDES LAKE DISTRICT

Introduction

Firstly, welcome to *Gravel Rides Lake District*. I wanted to create a guide that truly shows off gravel riding in its finest form in the stunning Lake District National Park. This wasn't always straightforward as the Lakes are so vast and we're not as blessed here, compared with some other parts of the UK, with an abundance of gravel in its truest form. There have been some very long days in the saddle to create this collection of routes – rest assured you can pick up this book safe in the knowledge that it will guide you around the very best routes in the area. I do believe all these routes I have created tie in aptly with what we know gravel riding to be: fun and adventurous!

Gravel riding has boomed in the last couple of decades, following its revival in the early 2000s in America. Consequently, cycling brands have been very keen to create the perfect tool to ride on gravel. Ultimately though, what we've always wanted is a vessel that can combine the higher speed and efficiency of road cycling with the capability and freedom to ride on the roughest and, in some cases, extremely technical terrain. Here I have done my best to adapt the 'one true discipline of cycling', as I like to call it, to the terrain that I have right on my own doorstep – all 2,362 square kilometres of the national park.

This guide has a ride for everyone of any ability – the shorter and easier routes are a great starting point, or you can just jump in and tackle one of the more challenging routes straight away if you've got the skills and experience. Take your time and remember, if you feel worried about anything technical, it's always okay to get off and push your bike!

I love gravel riding for its spirit of inclusivity. This genre of cycling accepts everyone from all walks of life – any bike or any shape or size, there are no egos here. We just want to ride bikes and be outside for as long as possible. This guide has been put together in the hope it will inspire others to get outside and enjoy the great outdoors.

Andrew Barlow

OPPOSITE MORECAMBE BAY.

Acknowledgements

This guide would have been much trickier to put together if I hadn't had help from a few individuals along the way. I would like to say a special thank you to those who have shared their opinions and recommendations with me.

Firstly, a big thank you to Ed Braithwaite and Rebecca Tatham at Lyon Equipment for supporting me with Salsa bikes, Ortlieb bike bags, Teravail tyres and equipment from Arundel. Being able to ride a bike which is more than a match for the tough Lake District terrain has been such a pleasure.

Thank you to everyone who has supported me with kit, clothing and everything in between: Nick Barlow, Jon Robinson, Adam Walton, Em Wormad, Jake Atkinson, Jimmy Mitchell, James Gossan, Rory Bell, Georgia Stevens, Jamie Cowan, Richard Smith, Georgie Burrows, James Dalton, Nick Day, Jack Peate, Jack Howard, Lottie Harman, Sarah Thornton, Biketreks and Wheelbase.

How to use this book
Riding in the Lake District

Gravel riding in the Lakes can be something of a mixed bag. There isn't the abundance of pristine gravel which you get in parts of Scotland, but this is more than compensated for by the variety of terrain you will encounter and the sensational, ever-changing views. These routes are on a mixture of gravel, unpaved roads, singletrack, forest tracks and roads – be prepared for tough ascents, bumpy descents and the odd beck crossing and boggy section.

The routes

This book contains 15 of the best gravel rides in the Lake District National Park. They vary in length from short, straightforward rides which you can squeeze into a busy day, to more hardcore, all-day and multi-day adventures which will truly test your skills as a rider.

Grades

The routes are split into sections by grade with the easiest routes in Section 1, moderate routes in Section 2 and the most challenging routes in Section 3.

Easy routes are suitable for all fitness and skill levels. They don't include any very steep sections, and the surfaces are mainly compacted gravel or solid earth with some smaller rocks, along with roads. The surface may become loose in some areas. Navigation is simple.

Straightforward routes are suitable for riders with a good level of fitness and more advanced riding skills. They may include steeper sections, either on roads or on trails. Surfaces may be a bit tougher, but still mainly rideable. Navigation is a little more involved.

Challenging routes are full-on adventures. You'll need to be fit and have excellent riding skills to get the most out of these routes. Surfaces can be loose with some larger obstacles, and there may be small sections of hike-a-bike. Navigation may require a bit more concentration.

Bear in mind that these grades are based on average conditions – all routes will be easier in good weather and harder in bad weather. Grades take into account not only the length of the route but the terrain, amount of climbing, navigational difficulty and how remote the route is. So, one challenging route could be short but very technical, whereas another could test your endurance and navigation skills. Your own fitness levels and technical ability will obviously influence how tricky you find the routes.

Directions & accuracy

While every effort has been made to ensure accuracy within the directions in this guide, things change and we are unable to guarantee that every detail will be correct. Please treat stated distances as guidelines. **Please exercise caution if a direction appears at odds with the route on the ground. A comparison between direction and map should see you on the right track.**

The GPX files provided (see page vii) can be easily uploaded on to a GPS device or smartphone to aid with navigation. GPS is usually reliable and accurate, but taking a paper map and compass and knowing how to use them is strongly recommended.

Rights of way

Countryside access in England hasn't been particularly kind to cyclists, although things are improving. We have 'right of way' on bridleways and byways. However, having 'right of way' doesn't actually mean having the right of way, just that we're allowed to ride there – so please give way to walkers and horse riders. We're also allowed to ride on green lanes and some unclassified roads, although the only way to determine which are legal and which aren't is to check with the local countryside authority. Obviously, cycle routes are also in.

The very understanding Forestry Commission generally allows cyclists to use its land (again, you'll need to check with them first to be sure). You must, however, obey all signs, especially those warning of forestry operations – a fully loaded logging truck will do more than scuff your frame …

Everything else is out of bounds (unless, of course, the landowner says otherwise).

Riding illegally can upset walkers (who have every right to enjoy their day) and is, in many cases, technically classed as trespass (meaning you could be prosecuted for any damage caused). Not all tracks are signed, so it's not always obvious whether that great-looking trail you want to follow is an 'illegal' footpath or a 'legal' bridleway. That's why it's a good idea to carry a map with you on every ride.

On the roads, cyclists are obliged to adhere to the Highway Code. Although no specific speed limits are applicable to cyclists, you may be charged with cycling carelessly or furiously. Cycling on pavements is illegal, unless it is also a cycle path. Helmets are not mandatory though we recommend you always wear one. At night, your bike must have a white front light and red rear light (flashing lights are permitted), and also needs to be fitted with a red rear reflector and amber pedal reflectors.

Bikepacking

Gravel riding and bikepacking are natural companions. Staying overnight is a great option if you want to take your time on the longer routes, or link together some of the shorter ones. A two- or three-day micro adventure like this can be done in a variety of different ways.

Staying in a hostel or B&B is the easiest option, as you only have to carry the bare essentials in addition to your usual day-ride kit. Alternatively, you could choose to stay in a bothy (you'll need a bit more kit for this). These unlocked shelters are situated in remote areas (mainly in Scotland, but there are a few in the Lake District) and are maintained by the Mountain Bothies Association. When using them please act considerately and make sure you take all your rubbish away with you. You can also donate to the charity to help towards maintenance costs. It's a good idea to carry a back-up shelter, in case the bothy is full! ***www.mountainbothies.org.uk***

Taking your own tent and staying on commercial campsites is another good alternative. Finally, wild camping – when done responsibly and with the landowner's permission – is another good and inexpensive option. You can choose to take a tent, bivvy bag or hammock; I love a hammock set-up, especially in the summer months. Wild camping in England is actually illegal but there is a compromise and a mutual respect between those who wild camp responsibly and the landowners. I get myself as far away from civilisation as I can before setting up camp, I arrive as late as possible and leave just after the sun has risen, ensuring that I leave no trace other than a flat patch of grass where my tent or bivvy has been. Further information about camping and wild camping in the national park can be found at ***www.lakedistrict.gov.uk/visiting/where-to-stay/wild-camping***

SALSA CYCLES' JOURNEYER.

The bike

These routes are rideable on any half-decent gravel bike. For maximum versatility, choose a tyre width of between 40 and 50 millimetres with either 700c or 650b wheels. I usually go for 650b, as my Salsa Fargo allows me to fit up to a 3-inch (75-millimetre) tyre allowing me to have a slow but super-plush ride. Most importantly, ensure that your bike is well maintained and in full working order – you will need to be able to shift efficiently on the climbs, be able to stop on the descents and roll along seamlessly with a good volume of air in your tyres. These routes could also be ridden on a cross-country bike or even a hardtail mountain bike; the road sections may be marginally slower but hey, we aren't here to break any records, we are here to have a good time for a long time.

Tubeless setup is another big win in my opinion, especially when riding on rough terrain; you can run lower pressures without the risk of getting pinch punctures, not to mention there is almost no faff when you have a puncture. Any punctures are either sealed by the sealant or fixed in a timely manner with plugs. No faff with inner tubes – hurrah!

As for brakes, I prefer hydraulic as they have much better stopping power than cable-actuated brakes. Hydraulic brakes also require less maintenance so they are a win-win all round.

Extremely efficient gearing is important when riding in the Lake District. Something over a one-to-one ratio will be extremely beneficial as there is a lot of climbing. In my smallest gears I run a 30/42T which gives me a ratio of 0.71 meaning that I am over a third more efficient thus making the climbing way more manageable. The bigger, the better in this instance. Your cadence may be higher but the resistance you will feel through the pedals will be considerably less.

The other ancillaries are mostly down to personal choice. I ride on clipless pedals as I find this gives me more efficiency while climbing and way more control while descending. The handlebars I use are Salsa Cowchippers, which are mildly flared, giving me more control, better contact on my brake levers and increased comfort on descents.

Recommended kit list

Now, I've always been the kind of individual who likes to be prepared for all eventualities, but this sometimes equates to having to take everything including the kitchen sink. To help avoid this, I've come up with a core kit list of what I take on my day rides (see right). This varies slightly depending on weather and terrain, but is a useful starting point.

Always check the weather forecast before your ride, but don't completely rely on it as you don't want to get caught out on a fellside in a sharp shower without a waterproof. Don't skimp on the tools and spare parts – and make sure you actually know how to use them before you set off. I tend to carry all of my kit in a frame or bar bag, as this is considerably better than carrying anything on my back. A top tube bag has me covered for most eventualities; if I need more room I add on a bar or saddle bag.

Clothing

Getting your clothing and 'layering system' dialled in is a vital task, especially if you want to stay comfortable. It took me a considerable amount of time to work out which layering system worked for me. I suggest using technical fabrics, which for the most part are made from either synthetics or wool, because these types of fabrics manage moisture far more efficiently than something like cotton, which would just absorb moisture and then become cold once you stop moving.

In the coldest conditions I wear a base layer, a synthetic jersey or wool shirt, an insulated jacket or gilet, and finally a breathable waterproof. The waterproof doubles up as a windbreaker so I usually use this to cut the windchill out on cooler days. A good pair of bib shorts/longs or shorts with a chamois is essential if you want to be kind to your behind – this will give you smiles for miles rather than wishing you were not riding at all. There are many different chamois on the market and it may take some time to find the perfect one for you, but in my mind, this is an absolute necessity.

Kit list
Safety
- Helmet
- Gloves
- High-vis jacket/belt
- First aid kit
- Food and drink
- Emergency sweets or energy gels
- Waterproof jacket and spare insulation layer
- Buff to double up as a helmet liner or face covering
- Fully charged phone and GPS device
- Map and compass if you're heading somewhere remote

Bike
- Good-quality multitool with a range of Allen keys
- Chain breaker (often on multitool)
- Spoke key (often on multitool)
- Screwdriver (often on multitool)
- Torx key (often on multitool)
- Knife
- Spare tube, pump and tyre levers
- Tubeless repair kit, CO_2 canisters and inflator (if needed)
- Spare rear mech hanger
- Chain links or quick links
- Brake pads
- Zip ties and duct tape
- Fully charged front and rear lights

General safety

The ability to read a map, navigate in poor visibility and to understand weather warnings is essential. Don't head out in bad weather, unless you're confident and capable of doing so.

Some of the routes described point you at tough climbs and steep descents that can potentially be very dangerous. Too much exuberance on a steep descent in the middle of nowhere and you could be in more than a spot of bother, especially if you're alone. Consider your limitations and relative fragility.

Be self-sufficient. Carry food and water, spares, a tube and a pump. Consider a first aid kit. Even if it's warm, the weather could turn, so take a wind/waterproof. Think about what could happen on an enforced stop. Pack lights if you could finish in the dark.

If you're riding solo, think about the seriousness of an accident – you might be without help for a very long time. Tell someone where you're going, when you'll be back and tell them once you are back. Take a mobile phone, but don't expect a signal. And **don't** call out the ambulance because you've grazed your knee.

Riding in a group is safer and often more fun, but don't leave slower riders too far behind and give them a minute for a breather when they've caught up. Allow extra time for a group ride, as you'll inevitably stop and chat. You might need an extra top if you're standing around for a while. Ride within your ability, make sure you can slow down fast and give way to other users. Bells might be annoying, but they work. If you can't bring yourself to bolt one on, a polite 'excuse me' should be fine. **On hot, sunny days, slap on some factor 30+ and we recommend that you always wear a helmet.**

In the event of an accident

In the event of an accident requiring immediate assistance, dial **999** or **112** and ask for **POLICE** and then (if you are in a remote location) **MOUNTAIN RESCUE**. If you can supply the emergency services with a grid reference of exactly where you are it should help to speed up their response time.

Emergency rescue by SMS text

Another option in the UK is contacting the emergency services by SMS text – useful if you have a low battery or intermittent signal, but you do need to register your phone first. To register, simply text 'register' to 999 and then follow the instructions in the reply. Do it now – it could save yours or someone else's life. *www.emergencysms.net*

Rules of the (off) road

1. Always ride on legal trails.
2. Ride considerately – give way to horses and pedestrians.
3. Don't spook animals.
4. Ride in control – you don't know who's around the next corner.
5. Leave gates as you find them – if you're unsure, shut them.
6. Keep the noise down.
7. Leave no trace – take home everything you took out.
8. Keep water sources clean – don't take toilet stops near streams.
9. Enjoy the countryside and respect its life and work.

DESCENDING FROM THE TOP OF ASKHAM FELL (ROUTE 06).

Planning your ride

1 Consider the ability and experience of each rider in your group. Check the weather forecast. How much time do you have available? Now choose your route.
2 Study the route description before setting off, and cross-reference it with the relevant map.
3 Bear in mind everything we've suggested about safety, clothing, spares and food and drink.
4 Get out there!

Maps & symbols

Ordnance Survey maps are the most commonly used, are easy to read and many people are happy using them. If you're not familiar with OS maps and are unsure of what the symbols mean, you can download a free map legend from *www.ordnancesurvey.co.uk*

We've included details of the relevant OS map for each route. To find out more about OS maps or to order maps please visit *www.ordnancesurvey.co.uk*

Here's a guide to the symbols and abbreviations we use on the maps and in our directions:

- **S** Route starting point
- **AS** Alternative starting point
- **OR** Optional route
- **2** Stage marker
- **64** Additional grid line numbers to aid navigation

Abbreviations used in route directions
L = Left
LH = Left-hand
R = Right
RH = Right-hand
SA = Straight Ahead

MAPS & SYMBOLS

PRISTINE GRAVEL ALONGSIDE RYDAL WATER (ROUTE 03).

EASY ROUTES

TRACK LEADING UP TO FORCE CRAG MINE.

01 FORCE CRAG MINE & THE COLEDALE VALLEY

17.4km/10.8 miles

Introduction

This short and sweet out-and-back ride is ideal for when you're short on time but need a quick blast of fresh air and exercise. Starting in Keswick, minor roads and a brief stint on the A66 take you through the villages of Portinscale and Braithwaite to the bottom of the Coledale Valley. Now for the fun bit – a ribbon of prime gravel hugs the side of the valley and runs away into the distance. The Coledale Beck bubbles to your left and the views of the surrounding mountains get gradually more dramatic as the kilometres tick past.

Grisedale Pike rises to your right as you ascend, Causey Pike is to your left as you look over the Coledale Beck, and Crag Hill heads the valley with Force Crag, which gives the mine its name, sitting underneath. Once you're at the head of this spectacular valley you'll arrive at Force Crag Mine – this was the last working metal mine in the Lake District when it closed in 1991. It is a Scheduled Monument, meaning it has real historical importance, along with being a geological Site of Special Scientific Interest: please treat it with respect. The National Trust occasionally runs open days to look round the processing mill; unfortunately, the underground tunnels have collapsed.

Because the surface of this track is so good, this ride is a great year-round option. As an added winter bonus, when the becks are in full spate they look incredible. In the summer, there are a few little dipping pools in the beck if you need to cool off. If you've got time to linger, there are few nicer places to spend your time. This ride can be linked with routes 05, 07, 08 or 14 for a bigger day out.

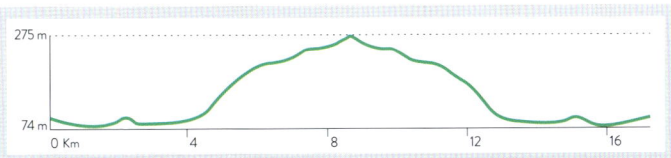

DISTANCE **17.4km/10.8 miles** — ASCENT **230m/755ft** — HIGHEST POINT **275m/900ft** — START/FINISH **Keswick** — START/FINISH GRID REF **NY 268234** — GPS **54.6012, -3.1346** — GRADE ■ — TERRAIN **Gravel; road; unpaved road** — PARKING **Various options in Keswick** — MAP **OS Landranger 89, West Cumbria; or 90, Penrith & Keswick (1:50,000)**

1 EEL CRAG. **2** THE FIRST AND ONLY GATE ALONG THIS TRACK. **3** WHATEVER THE WEATHER, ALWAYS KEEP HYDRATED.

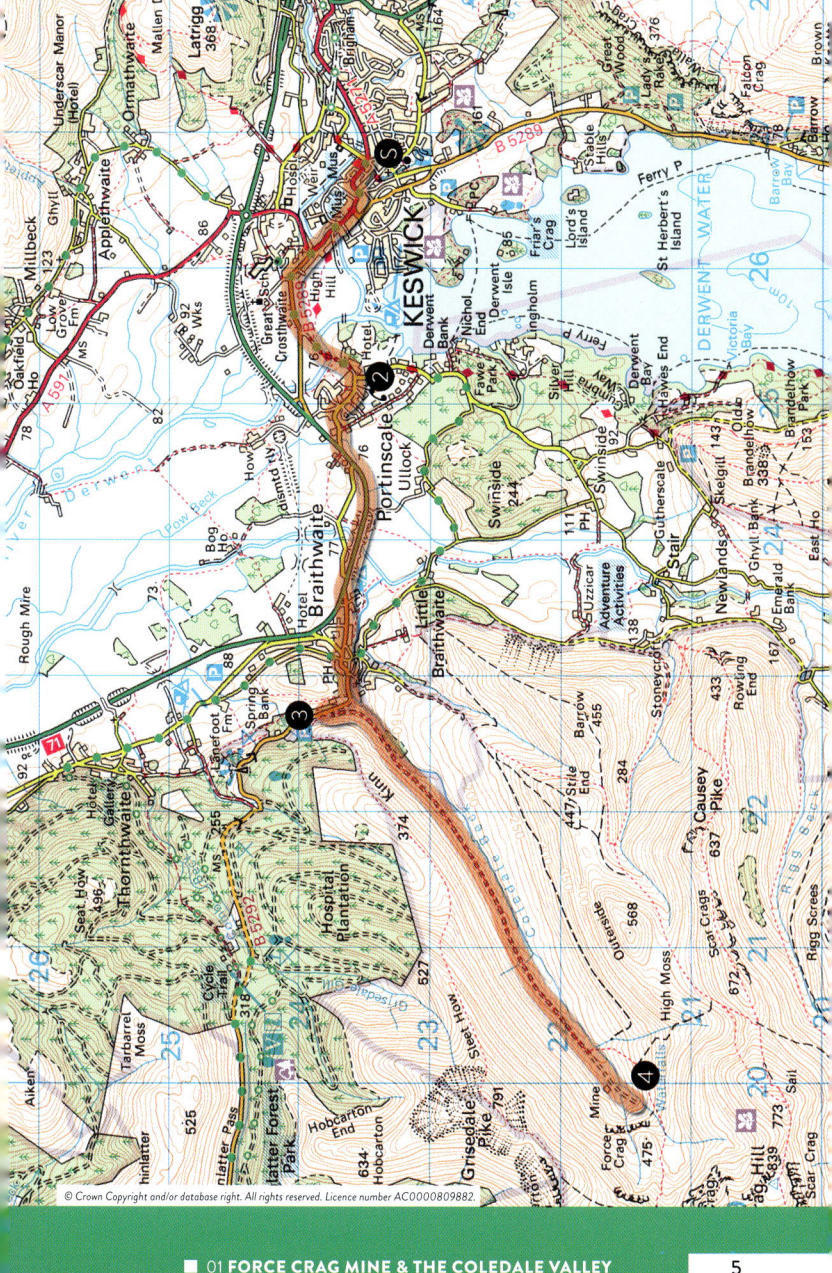

01 FORCE CRAG MINE & THE COLEDALE VALLEY

Directions

S Head west out of Keswick on the A5271. Cross the River Greta and keep left on the B5289 (also NCN route 71). After a few hundred metres turn **L** at a junction signed as a dead end road (still following NCN route 71) then dismount to cross an iron bridge over the River Derwent. Go **SA** on to a road and continue on, passing the Derwentwater Hotel, to reach a junction in Portinscale.

2 Turn **R**, following the signpost for *Keswick* and *Cockermouth*. Pass the Farmers Arms then turn **L** on to a cycle path which runs alongside the A66 (following the signpost for *Workington*, *Cockermouth* and *Braithwaite*). Follow the cycle path round to the **L** then follow the B5292 into Braithwaite. Carry on **SA** through the village passing the Royal Oak and continue until you reach a small car park on the left. (This car park can make a decent alternative start point, but it shortens the ride and is popular, so you have to get there early or late in the day.)

Coffee and food
Fellpack, Lake Road Brunch, The Square Orange or Cafe West, Keswick.

Bike shops
Biketreks, Keswick.

4 GOOD TRACK TO THE MINES. **5** CLIMBING UP THE TRACK LEADING TO THE MINES. **6** SANTA CRUZ STIGMATA.

3 Turn **L** through the car park and go through the barrier, following the signpost for *Force Crag Mine*. It's a footpath on the map, but the National Trust permits cycling. You're now on a gravel track climbing all the way to the head of the valley. The climbing is sustained, but as you gain height you get fantastic views of Coledale Beck and the surrounding mountains. Head through the gate and cross a little beck. Continue on to reach the mine buildings and pools underneath Force Crag.

4 Once you've spent some time exploring the site, retrace your steps to return to Keswick. The descent down the valley is super fun; there is little to no effort required on your return journey, just watch out for the 'speed bumps' in the track. Also be aware that this is a multi-recreational route so watch out for others enjoying the trail.

■ 01 **FORCE CRAG MINE & THE COLEDALE VALLEY**

HIGHEST POINT ON BLAWITH COMMON – ALL DOWNHILL FROM HERE.

02 **BLAWITH COMMON**
17.4km/10.8 miles

Introduction

Starting in the old mining village of Coniston, this ride passes by the ancient village of Torver, before a pleasant road section along the shore of Coniston Water. Then the fun begins – a stiff climb up a farm road on to Blawith Common before a lumpy and bumpy track takes you through this unique landscape. A descent down to Coniston Water follows before another stint on the shoreline – this time on the Cumbria Way – takes you back to Coniston in time for a brew.

Unfortunately, I feel like most of us in this day and age are always tied to the constraints of time. Luckily, this short ride gives a great sense of adventure without straying too far from civilisation. I encourage you to take this ride slowly if you can – vistas over to the Old Man of Coniston, Dow Crag and Wetherlam are just some that can be enjoyed. This area is slightly less on the main tourist trail than other parts of the Lakes so you may find some much-needed peace and quiet on this ride.

Blawith Common really feels wild and rugged. It's very rare in the Lake District to find yourself riding over an expanse of land like this – you'll see exactly what I mean once you are up there. The terrain on this ride covers it all – from prime gravel and tarmac to some rougher tracks. The most challenging parts are across the common where it's lumpy and bumpy; also during the wetter months it can become a bit of a quagmire.

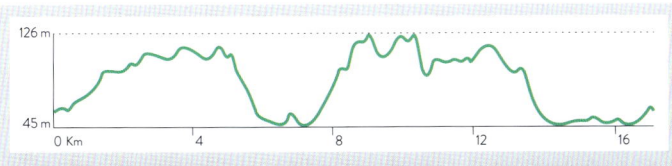

DISTANCE **17.4km/10.8 miles** ▬ ASCENT **200m/655ft** ▬ HIGHEST POINT **126m/415ft** ▬ START/FINISH **Coniston** ▬ START/FINISH GRID REF **SD 302975** ▬ GPS **54.3690, -3.0757** ▬ GRADE ■ ▬ TERRAIN **Road; bridleway; unpaved road** ▬ PARKING **Lots of options in Coniston; Coniston Sports and Social Centre (parking charge; grid reference SD 305977) is a good choice** ▬ MAP **OS Landranger 96, Barrow-in-Furness & South Lakeland; or 97, Kendal & Morecambe (1:50,000)**

1 A PUSH AND A SHOVE UP OVER THE LUMPY PARTS TO THE TOP OF THE COMMON. **2** CONISTON OLD MAN AND DOW CRAG. **3** BRIDLEWAY RUNNING NEXT TO THE DISUSED RESERVOIR.

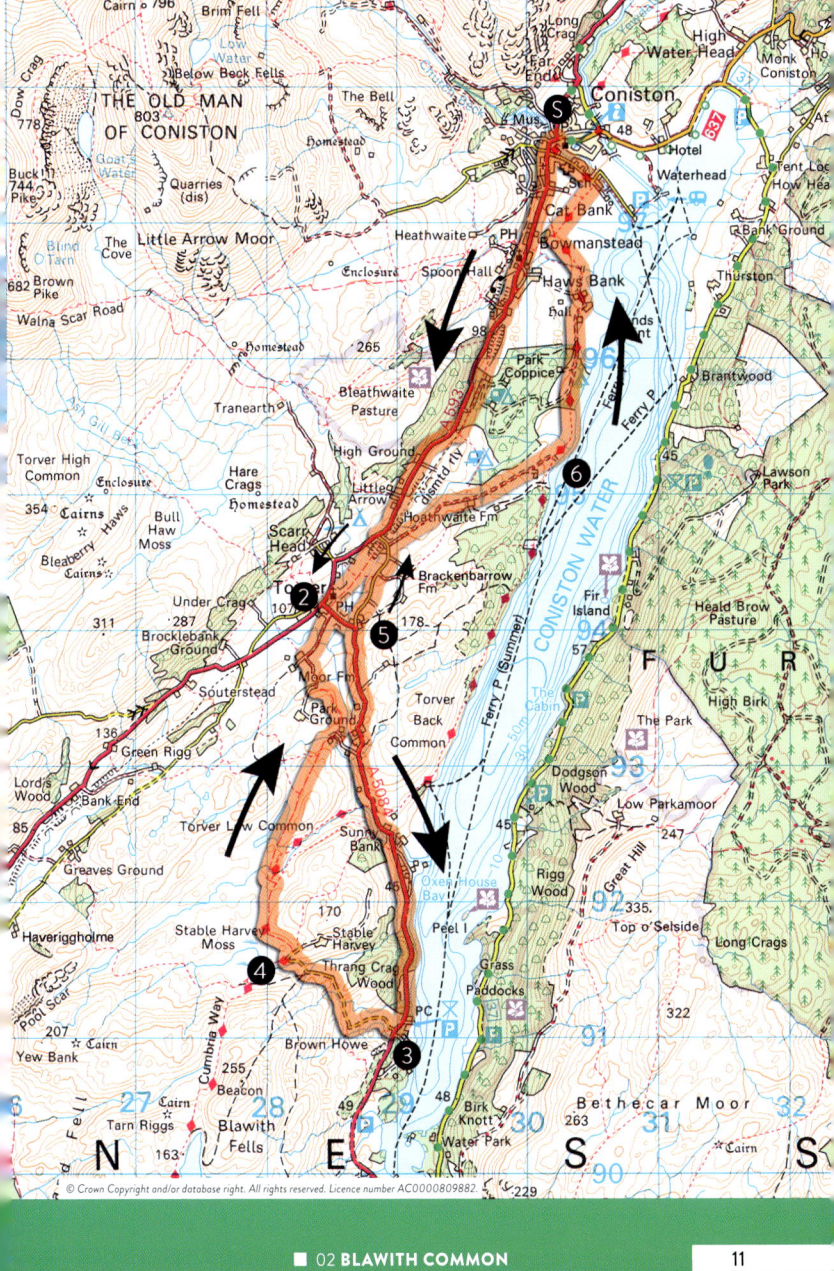

02 BLAWITH COMMON

11

Directions

S Leave Coniston on the A593, heading south in the direction of Broughton and Ulverston. Pass through Bowmanstead and Haws Bank then at a bend bear **L** on to a cycle trail (signposted *Torver*). This runs parallel to the main road and it's possible to avoid riding on the road all the way to Torver. The route passes through Park Coppice and always keeps to the left of the road passing through various gates along the way; in some places it's separated from the road by a wall, while for a short section there's some singletrack near the road. After passing through more gates the final section follows the old railway more distinctly and then emerges at the A5084 in Torver.

2 Turn **L** on to the A5084. This fun road descent takes you past Kelly Hall Tarn to reach the shore of Coniston Water. Follow the road along then away from the shoreline, passing Brown Howe car park to reach a junction a short distance after the car park.

3 Turn **R** up the dead-end road that starts your climb up to Blawith Common. The climb is short and steep but manageable; it winds its way up through some coppices before it opens up into common land which is mainly used for sheep grazing. Continue to almost the end of the road, just before the gate to Stable Harvey.

Coffee and food
The Green Housekeeper, Coniston; Undercrag Cafe, Torver.

Bike shops
Ghyllside Cycles or Push Cartel, Ambleside; Biketreks, Grizedale Forest.

4 SHORT AND STEEP ROAD CLIMB. **5** RIDING THROUGH MERE BECK. **6** VISTA OVER THE CONISTON RANGE.

4 Turn **L** here, following the *Public Bridleway* fingerpost. The singletrack meanders through the common; pay close attention to the map or GPX here, there are *Public Bridleway* fingerposts in places to point you in the right direction too. Ground-nesting birds such as lapwing and skylark can be seen and heard, as views of common land make way for the mountain landscape. Pass the disused Throng Moss Reservoir then head down the grassy descent towards Mill Bridge. Go through a gate and continue down a rough bridleway to reach a couple of houses and a driveway; bear **L**, keeping Torver Beck on your right. Keep following the bridleway, turning **R** and **R** again to reach the A5084 in Torver. Turn **R** and follow the A5084 for 250m.

5 Turn **L**, following the signpost saying *Single track road*. Continue for around 800m then turn **R**, heading towards Hoathwaite Farm. Descend past the farm towards Coniston Water.

6 Bear **L** to join the Cumbria Way, heading north along the shoreline. This is a really enjoyable part of the ride and also a perfect spot for a dip in the warmer months of the year. Keep following the well-signposted Cumbria Way through a couple of farms and boatyards back towards Coniston. Be mindful that in peak season this prime piece of gravel will likely be busy with walkers and families, so be kind, say hello and give priority to other users. Turn **L** along Lake Road and then turn **R** along Broughton Road to return to the centre of Coniston.

RIDING ALONG LOUGHRIGG TERRACE.

03 **LOUGHRIGG LOOP**
18.1km/11.2 miles

Introduction

This route is a lap of possibly one of the most underrated fells in the entire Lake District National Park and it's a ride that I do on almost a monthly basis when I want something that's super chilled with quintessential Lake District views and prime gravel. The amalgamation of bridleway and minor roads gives this ride a great balance and opens doors for those looking at getting into gravel riding as almost all of this route is ridable (take the alternative route south of Loughrigg Tarn to avoid the roughest stuff). Just a couple of punchy climbs and questionable paving or drainage ditches to contend with. Not to mention that there's astounding views throughout the entirety of this ride.

The route starts in Ambleside and passes through Rothay Park; when I first moved to the Lakes this is the park where I'd walk my dog, spend my lunch hour and many a sunny evening soaking in the surrounding landscape. You're soon on a quiet minor road alongside the River Rothay, before passing the southern shore of Rydal Water. Continuing on the rocky bridleway along Loughrigg Terrace (take in the stunning views here), you're soon heading into Elterwater village before more bridleways and quiet roads take you back past Loughrigg Tarn to Ambleside.

There's one place in particular on this ride that has special memories for me: the Britannia Inn in Elterwater village. My first memory of the Lake District is coming on holiday here and staying at the Brit with Mum, Dad, my twin brother and the dogs. I remember sitting outside here enjoying a bar meal on the only day of sunshine of the entire week we were in the Lakes – no surprise there in the slightest!

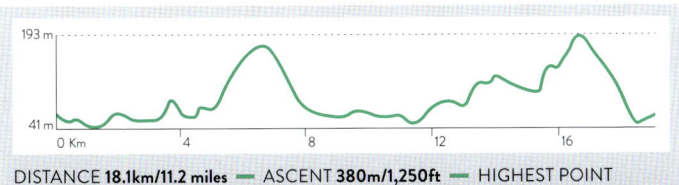

DISTANCE **18.1km/11.2 miles** — ASCENT **380m/1,250ft** — HIGHEST POINT **193m/635ft** — START/FINISH **Ambleside** — START/FINISH GRID REF **NY 376045** — GPS **54.4323, -2.9623** — GRADE ■ — TERRAIN **Gravel; road; unpaved road** — PUBLIC TRANSPORT **Ambleside bus interchange** — PARKING **Various options in Ambleside** — MAP **OS Landranger 90, Penrith & Keswick (1:50,000)**

1 THIS WAY TO LANGDALE. **2** ELTER WATER. **3** GOOD GRAVEL ALONGSIDE ELTER WATER.

03 LOUGHRIGG LOOP

17

Directions

S Starting at the market cross in Ambleside, head east along Rydal Road then turn **R** on to Church Street. Turn **R** on to Compston Road, rejoining the one-way system. Turn **L** on to Millans Park and then immediately **L** on to Vicarage Road. Continue **SA** past the school into Rothay Park, aptly named as the River Rothay runs round the park.

2 Once through the park and over the bridge, turn **R** over a cattle grid on to the Under Loughrigg road (also NCN route 6), skirting the eastern side of Loughrigg Fell through rolling lowlands and old woodlands by the river. Pass some stepping stones and go over another cattle grid then turn **L** towards Pelter Bridge car park. There is a short climb past some cottages (look out for the honesty box which usually has some baking) then the road turns into a prime gravel track; once through the gate, keep **R** to ride along the southern shores of Rydal Water – it's a great spot for a swim if you fancy it.

3 Keep **L**, uphill, heading west towards Grasmere. The crowds start to disperse as you climb up along Loughrigg Terrace. The views open out over Grasmere with Silver How, Tarn Crag, Seat Sandal and Stone Arthur framing the mere perfectly. A steady yet rocky climb takes you to the road at Red Bank, which is a well-known climb out of Grasmere.

4 Turn **L** along Red Bank then fork **R**, following the signpost for *Langdales* and *YHA*. It's a short pull up to the hostel before a drop over a cattle grid where the views open up into Langdale. Snake your way down the side of the fell on a fast and fun road section (keeping sharp **L** at one point) to come to a crossroads with the main Langdale road; go **SA** into Elterwater village to reach the Britannia Inn.

5 Continue past the pub then turn **L** into a car park, following the signpost for *Ambleside*. Go through the gate and follow the trail with Great Langdale Beck on your right. The first section to Elter Water is cobbled and mucky when wet; this surface is short-lived, and it soon turns into that fine, hard-packed gravel we all know and love.

6 After about 2km the trail passes through a gate into woodland near Skelwith Force. Shortly, turn **R** over an impressive metal bridge, following the signed NCN route 37. Follow this through woodland, bearing **L** to a gate (ahead is a footpath) and then through another gate near a house to join the A593. Turn **L** and cruise downhill into Skelwith Bridge. Chesters by the River is just over the bridge on the left if you need to refuel.

4 THIS WAY TO CHESTERS.

Coffee and food
Copper Pot or The Apple Pie, Ambleside; Chesters by the River, Skelwith Bridge; Britannia Inn, Elterwater.

Bike shops
Ghyllside Cycles or Push Cartel, Ambleside.

7 Turn **L** on to the B5343 (either from the A593 or the buildings by Chesters). Continue along the road as you slowly ascend, then turn **R** on to the minor road after approximately 1.5km. Turn **R** at the top of this progressive climb, pass a copse of trees then turn **L**. Pass through a farm and continue until you reach a gated bridleway signposted *Loughrigg Tarn* on your right.

8 Turn **R** on to the bridleway to enjoy the premium gravel around Loughrigg Tarn. This is a great spot where you can stop, swim or simply take in the surrounding views.

9 Continue around the tarn to reach a bridleway junction at Tarn Foot.* Turn **L** on to another bridleway. Following your nose, this soon becomes steep in sections with parts where it may be necessary to push. Along this climb there's a couple of big drainage ditches, so go steady and keep your eyes open for them. Go through the beck and up the final pull – you'll have a view down Windermere, over to Coniston and the fells beyond. Now for the fun part, the descent. Keep **R** and you'll come over a short section of the lumpy bumpy stuff; watch for drainage ditches here. Then there's a short section of smooth gravel before dropping into a steep rougher section to reach a gate. Go through the gate and you're now on the final decent; the bridleway turns into a tarmac road around halfway down. Caution is advised as it is a popular walking route and there's a hairpin corner. Continue to meet a road. Turn **R** on to the road then turn **L** over the bridge and follow your outward route back through the park into Ambleside.

OR *Alternatively, to miss out the potential hike-a-bike, turn **R** then turn **L** on to a road. Turn **L** on to the A593 and follow this back to Ambleside.

■ 03 **LOUGHRIGG LOOP**

VIEWS OVER TO THE LANGDALE PIKES FROM CLAIFE HEIGHTS.

04 AMBLESIDE, HAWKSHEAD & CLAIFE HEIGHTS

26.6km/16.5 miles

Introduction

I feel this route takes me back to the very roots of why I moved to the Lake District; the enticing views that had me questioning what's down in that valley or beyond that summit, encouraging me to explore. I've found myself more often than not heading in the initial direction of this route in search of the perfect way to keep off the beaten track and to really enjoy the quiet corners. In search of what exactly I'm unsure, but it gives me the feeling I had when I was a kid, just riding my bike and seeing where I ended up.

There are many possible routes in this area, but I feel this is the best amalgamation I could piece together for sightseeing and soaking up the quintessential Lake District gravel riding. This route starts in the popular village of Ambleside and rolls through the quaint village of Hawkshead with its cobbled streets, cute cafes and cat-bar. Moving on past Esthwaite Water to the hamlet of Near Sawrey, you can visit Beatrix Potter's house for a cuppa with Peter Rabbit and Benjamin Bunny, and then Moss Eccles Tarn, which is said to have been one of her favourite places within the Lakes. There's then a climb through the woodland of Claife Heights, before descending back to Ambleside.

I prefer this ride at either extreme of the day. The quieter it is the better – you'll feel secluded and immersed but, in actual fact, you're not that far from anywhere so it's perfect for those days where you may want to ride more slowly and just take it all in. There are some great places to stop off too – there's always time for another coffee …

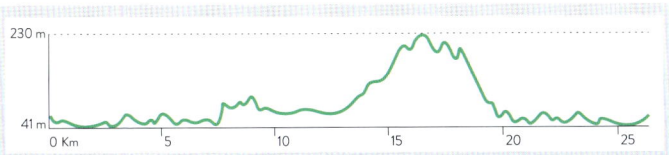

DISTANCE **26.6km/16.5 miles** — ASCENT **360m/1,180ft** — HIGHEST POINT **230m/750ft** — START/FINISH **Ambleside** — START/FINISH GRID REF **NY 376045** — GPS **54.4323, -2.9623** — GRADE ■ — TERRAIN **Hard-packed gravel; tarmac; rough bridleway** — PUBLIC TRANSPORT **Ambleside bus interchange** — PARKING **Various options in Ambleside** — MAP **OS Landranger 90, Penrith & Keswick; 97, Kendal & Morecambe (1:50,000)**

1

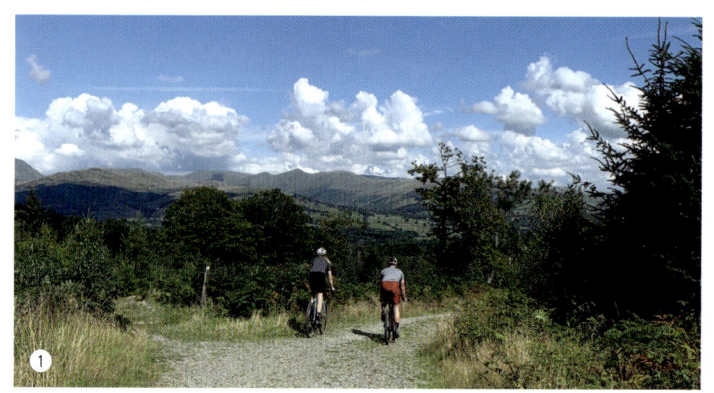

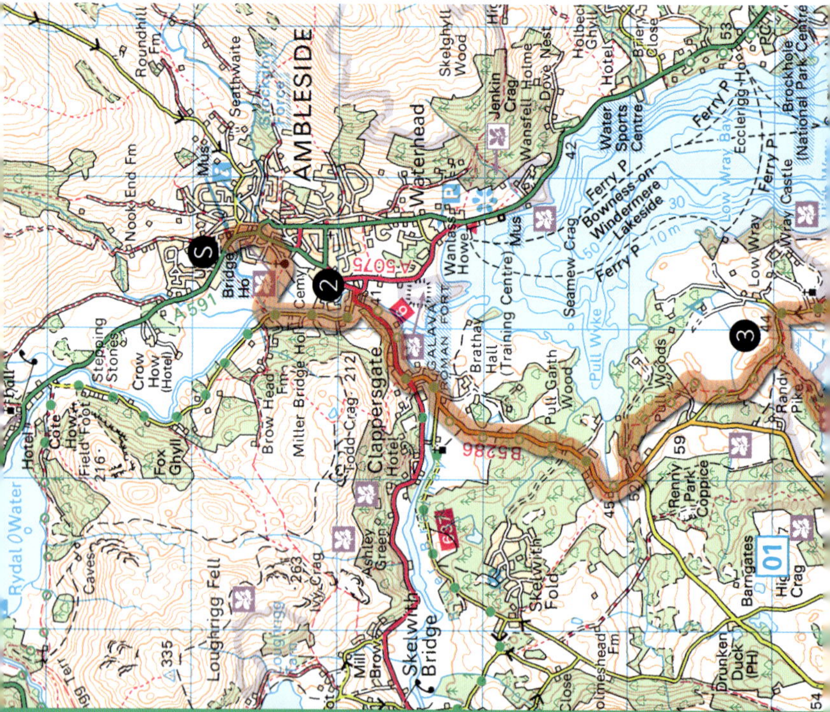
AMBLESIDE
Waterhead
Wansfell Holme
Jenkin Crag
Skelghyll Wood
Roundhill Fm
Seathwaite
Stock Ghyll Force
Nook End Fm
Stepping Stones
Crow How (Hotel)
Brow Head Fm
Miller Bridge Ho
Clappersgate
Todd Crag 212
Fox Ghyll
Field Foot
Rydal Water
Caves
Loughrigg Fell
335
263
Ivy Crag
Ashley Green
Skelwith Bridge
Mill Brow
Skelwith Fold
Brathay Hall (Training Centre)
GALAVA ROMAN FORT
Wanlass Howe
Seamew Crag
Pull Wyke
Pull Garth Wood
Pull Woods
Bowness-on-Windermere Lakeside
Ferry P
Water Sports Centre
Low Wray Bay
Ecclerigg Ho
Brockhole National Park Centre
Wray Castle
Low Wray
Randy Pike
Renny Park Coppice
Barngates
Drunken Duck (PH)
High Crag
Holbeck Ghyll
Briery Close
Dove Nest
A591
A5075
B5286
S
2
3
01

1 DECENDING THE GRAVEL DOWN TO BASECAMP. **2** VIEWS OVER COLTHOUSE HEIGHTS WITH THE CONISTON RANGE IN FULL VIEW.

■ 04 **AMBLESIDE, HAWKSHEAD & CLAIFE HEIGHTS**   23

Directions

S Starting at the market cross in Ambleside, head east along Rydal Road then turn **R** on to Church Street. Turn **R** on to Compston Road, rejoining the one-way system. Turn **L** on to Millans Park and then immediately **L** on to Vicarage Road. Continue **SA** past the school into Rothay Park. Once through the park and over the bridge, turn **L** on to the quiet road of Under Loughrigg to reach a junction with the A593.

2 Turn **R** on to the A593, following the signpost for *Skelwith Bridge* and *Coniston*, then bear **L** on to the cycle path which runs alongside the road. Turn **L** on to the B5286, following the signpost for *Hawkshead* and crossing the River Brathay. Just after a turn-off on the right, bear **R** on to a cycleway (NCN route 6) which runs alongside the road. It crosses from one side of the road to the other near Skelwith Fold Caravan Park, and then joins the road for a short section near the entrance to Pull Wyke; rejoin the signed cycleway after emerging from the trees. Stay with NCN route 6 as it veers away from the road, gently climbing through Pull Woods to reach a gate where views open up to Hawkshead Hill to the south-west. Go through a gate and descend then go through a couple more gates to meet the road. Cross the road and continue on the cycleway for a short time to reach a junction.

3 Turn **R** at the junction, heading towards Blelham Tarn. This next section of gravel doubletrack is super smooth, and it flows really nicely; follow this through fields and woodland, keeping right near High Tock How and left at Birkwray Farm, to meet a minor road near Loanthwaite. Turn **R** on to the road; after 200m turn **L** on to Scar House Lane then after 300m fork **R** on to a bridleway to meet the B5285 in Hawkshead. (Detour into the village to refuel if you need to.)

3 WISE EEN TARN. **4** PUSHING UP THE ROUGH STUFF PAST MOSS ECCLES TARN. **5** DECENDING THE GRAVEL OF CLAIFE HEIGHTS.

Coffee and food
Copper Pot, Ambleside; Kittchen, Hawkshead; Joey's, Wray Castle; Drunken Duck Inn, Barngates.

Bike shops
Push Cartel or Ghyllside Cycles, Ambleside; Biketreks, Grizedale Forest.

❹ Turn **L** on to the B5285 – this road section soon brings you alongside Esthwaite Water then on into the hamlet of Near Sawrey, famous for Hill Top, Beatrix Potter's house.

❺ Turn **L** on to Stones Lane – this goes through a farm then becomes a good bridleway which climbs to Moss Eccles Tarn and on to Claife Heights. This climb is enjoyable, however you may have to get off and push in some instances because it is really rough in some places, especially after the tarn. There is also a small beck to cross – go steady in the wetter months as this can be surprisingly deep; it has caught me out before. You've done the hard work, now it's time to enjoy yourself. At the top of the climb you'll find yourself immersed in a conifer plantation – it's now time for an absolute treat of a fire road descent all the way to the road in High Wray. Pay close attention to the map or GPX here, as there are lots of tracks in the forest. Note once you've gone through the gate at Basecamp this section of fire road sometimes has vehicle traffic on it.

❻ Turn **R** on to the road at High Wray and continue for around 1km to reach the gatehouse for Wray Castle (turn right here if you wish to detour to the castle or cafe). Shortly after the gatehouse, bear **L** on to a cycle path (NCN route 6) following the signpost for *Ambleside*. After around 200m this brings you to the junction at point ❸; turn **R** to retrace your route back to Ambleside.

■ 04 **AMBLESIDE, HAWKSHEAD & CLAIFE HEIGHTS**

ADMIRING THE LANGDALE PIKES NEAR THE TOP OF BLEA TARN PASS (ROUTE 09).

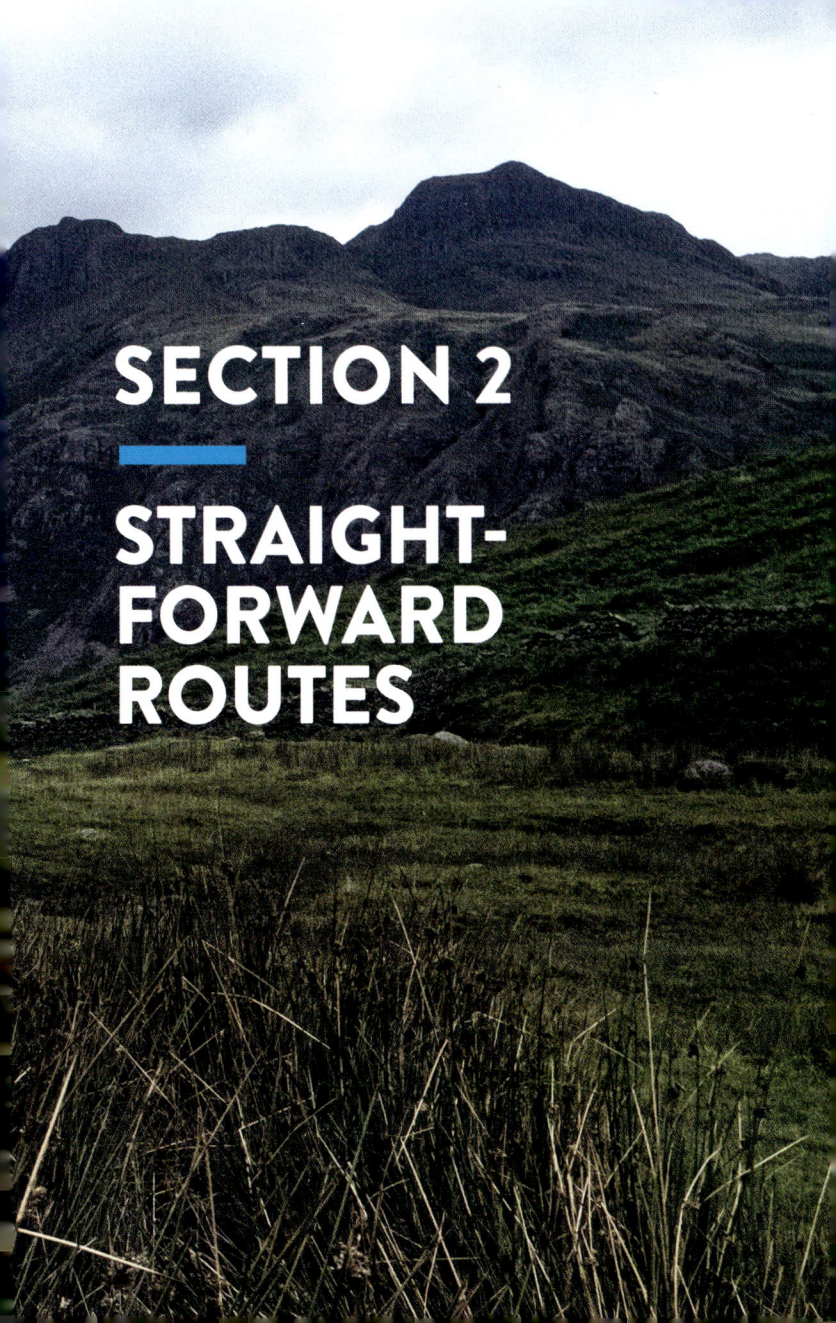

SECTION 2

STRAIGHT-FORWARD ROUTES

LOOKING OVER TO BLENCATHRA.

05 ST JOHN'S IN THE VALE & KESWICK RAILWAY PATH

19.3km/12 miles

Introduction

This is one of those rides to enjoy if you're a little short on time. You're never too far from civilisation and it offers some truly stunning views in exchange for little effort. The terrain is a mix of gravel trails, bridleways and roads, with a few sections of more technical singletrack and deeper gravel to test your skills.

Starting from Keswick, the first section of the route takes you east on a disused railway line. Now a popular, five-kilometre ribbon of tarmac, this is part of an old railway that ran from Cockermouth to Penrith. This multi-use path can be better in the early mornings or evenings, when it's quieter. After crossing the A66, the route takes you south on to some quiet back lanes to reach St John's in the Vale, a picturesque, glacial valley dotted with farms. Even in the height of summer,

I've never passed many other people here. There are great views of the Helvellyn mountain range as you drop down into the valley – Clough Head and Great Dodd stand tall.

Moving on, you cross St John's Beck and head over fields to reach one of my favourite bridleways which contours around High Rigg to reach St John's Church. This narrow path really feels like a singletrack roller coaster, and a fairly technical, steep climb at the end has some deep gravel to really test the best riders. The views are unreal as you pass the church and ride in between Low Rigg and High Rigg. Some more quiet roads take you to the A591, then a climb and a fast descent take you back into Keswick for a post-ride beverage.

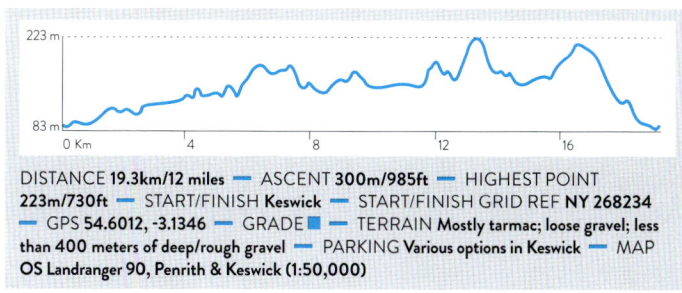

DISTANCE **19.3km/12 miles** — ASCENT **300m/985ft** — HIGHEST POINT **223m/730ft** — START/FINISH **Keswick** — START/FINISH GRID REF **NY 268234** — GPS **54.6012, -3.1346** — GRADE ■ — TERRAIN **Mostly tarmac; loose gravel; less than 400 meters of deep/rough gravel** — PARKING **Various options in Keswick** — MAP **OS Landranger 90, Penrith & Keswick (1:50,000)**

1 LOOKING OVER TO CLOUGH HEAD. 2 START OF THE OFF-ROAD SECTION.

05 ST JOHN'S IN THE VALE & KESWICK RAILWAY PATH   31

Directions

S Head north out of Keswick, crossing the River Greta on Station Road. Where the road curves to the right, go **SA** on to a cycle path (NCN route 71). Bear **R** to join the old railway line; continue for 5km to reach the A66.

2 Turn **L** on to the A66; shortly afterwards turn **R** (staying with NCN route 71 and following the signpost for *Castlerigg Stone Circle* and *Burns Farm*). Take the next **L** turn (following the signpost for *St John's in the Vale*) – this is a really fast descent, watch out for some tight corners. Cross St John's Beck and continue until you reach a T-junction with the B5322. (Notice the size of Clough Head in front of you; the Helvellyn range can truly make you feel small at times.)

3 Turn **R** on to the B5322 through St John's in the Vale. After 2.3km turn **R** (going back on yourself) on to a bridleway. Cross a stone bridge then go through a gate and head diagonally **R** across a field, heading for a gate in the middle of the wall. Go through the gate then turn **R** on to a bridleway underneath High Rigg.

Coffee and food
Fellpack, Lake Road Brunch,
The Square Orange or Cafe West,
Keswick.

Bike shops
Biketreks, Keswick.

3 GRASSY BRIDLEWAY HEADING BACK TOWARDS KESWICK. **4** VIEWS LOOKING DOWN ST JOHN'S IN THE VALE.

Climb, descend then climb again on the bridleway (there is also some really nice singletrack and some technical, lumpy, tree root climbs, with deeper parts of gravel) before you pop out on to a road near St John's Church.

4 Turn **L** on to the road and keep climbing to reach the church. Continue **SA** on to a gravel track, which sits between High Rigg and Low Rigg, to start the descent. Parts of this 4x4 track are a little sketchy (I once had a spectacular crash down here) and there are some very deep sections of gravel that you can easily wash out on. Go round a couple of zigzags to reach a narrow road. Turn **L** on to the road.

5 After 600m turn **R** through a gate on to a road passing through Naddle to reach the A591. Turn **R** on to the A591 (this section can be busy but the road is nice and wide) for a last climb then a super-fast descent into Keswick. Turn **L** on to Manor Brow (signposted *Castlerigg Manor*), turn **R** on to Eskin Street, go **SA** on to Greta Street and finally turn **L** on to Penrith Road to get back to your starting point.

■ 05 **ST JOHN'S IN THE VALE & KESWICK RAILWAY PATH**

VIEWS OVER ULLSWATER TO HELVELLYN.

06 ASKHAM FELL

20.4km/12.7 miles

Introduction

Courses of old Roman roads, stone circles, views towards Helvellyn and a fun descent towards Ullswater – this ride has it all. It doesn't matter if it's blowing a hoolie or a beautiful blue sky summer's day, this ride is one to go for; it's short and sweet but gives you everything you need to feel fulfilled. The climbing is steady so you can really sit back and take in your surroundings. Take your time descending because the views are absolutely out of this world – there are some real 'pinch me' moments.

Starting in the village of Askham – best known for its proximity to Lowther Castle (worth a stop if you have time) – you're soon away from civilisation and heading west out on to Askham Fell. There are a couple of interesting landmarks up here. The route crosses the course of High Street, a Roman road which runs between Ambleside and Brougham Fort near Penrith. Just next to the crossing with High Street you'll see a Bronze Age stone circle known as The Cockpit.

Next there is a fun descent underneath Barton Fell to Ullswater. The road along the shoreline is peaceful and scenic, and there are opportunities to get down to the water for a swim if you fancy it – highly recommended but be aware that Ullswater has a reputation as one of the coldest lakes in the Lake District! This road leads to the outskirts of Pooley Bridge, a great place to stop if you need some fuel for the final climb over Heughscar Hill back to Askham.

This is a great ride no matter what the weather. I would say it's better in the drier months of the year (wishful thinking in Cumbria) but out of season it's a ride where you'll barely see another soul.

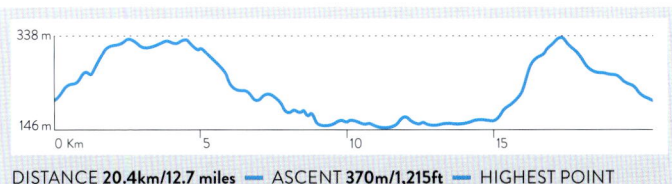

DISTANCE **20.4km/12.7 miles** — ASCENT **370m/1,215ft** — HIGHEST POINT **338m/1,110ft** — START/FINISH **Askham** — START/FINISH GRID REF **NY 512236** — GPS **54.6058, -2.7557** — GRADE ■ — TERRAIN **Singletrack; road; paved track; gravel** — PARKING **Small car park in Askham or park at nearby Lowther Castle and make use of the cafe** — MAP **OS Landranger 90, Penrith & Keswick (1:50,000)**

1 HEADING TOWARDS THE STONE CIRCLE.

Directions

S Head west out of Askham on a minor road and continue **SA** as it becomes a bridleway. This climbs gently, first on gravel then on to nice, flowing grassy trails on the plateau, to reach a stone circle known as The Cockpit.

2 Continue **SA** on the bridleway (High Street, a Roman road, crosses the route here). This turns into a bit of rougher singletrack and heads underneath Barton Fell for the descent towards Ullswater. You will be slowed down sometimes due to the bridleway being quite rough in places, but the descent to Howtown is a treat and is the best part of 5km long.

3 Cross a footbridge and turn **R** to reach the road in Howtown. Turn **R** on to the road and cycle for 6km along the shore of Ullswater to reach a crossroads on the edge of Pooley Bridge. (Detour into the village for refreshments if needed, but don't go over the top as there is a tough climb ahead!)

4 Turn **R**; after 1km continue **SA** on to a bridleway. Turn **L** shortly afterwards to begin a climb on a bridleway that runs up the side of Heughscar Hill. Just after you start to descend, turn **L** on to a track near a farm then turn **R** to meet a road. Turn **R** on to the road then turn **R** again to return to Askham.

Coffee and food
Lowther Castle Cafe or Askham Stores, Askham; Granny Dowbekin's, Pooley Bridge.

Bike shops
Arragon's Cycles, Penrith.

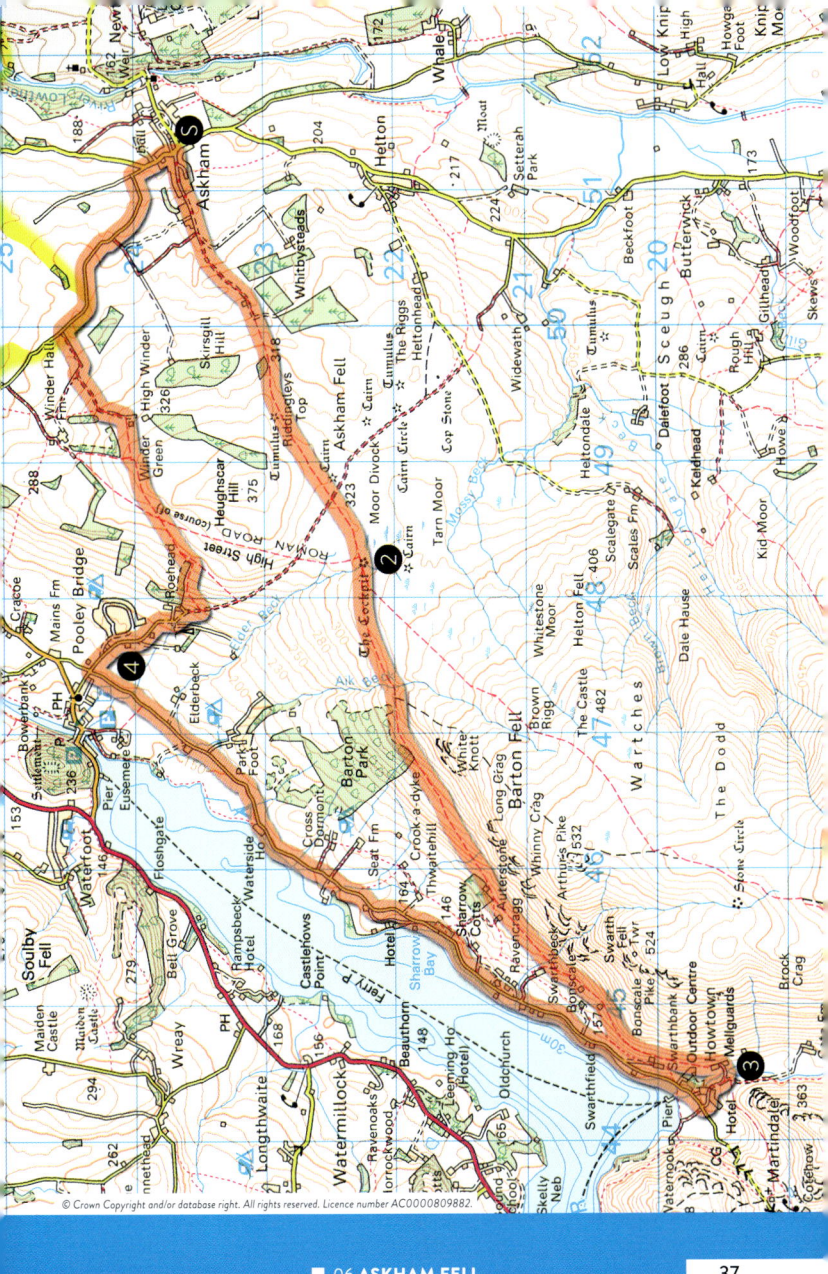

GRAVEL TO SKIDDAW HOUSE. © JOHN COEFIELD.

07 **GLENDERATERRA**

18.4km/11.4 miles

Introduction

I always describe Glenderaterra as a route with four distinct parts. Starting in the bustling town of Keswick, the first part of the ride transports you to Threlkeld first via a disused railway then up past some Cumbrian farms. The second part sees you heading out along the Glenderaterra Beck and making your way to the head of the valley between Lonscale Fell and Blease Fell before joining the renowned Cumbria Way along the other side of the beck and around the side of Lonscale Fell. On a clear day you'll be able to see Helvellyn, Great Gable and Grisedale Pike.

The third part is my favourite as you make your way around Latrigg. Just off route, this is one of the smaller yet most accessible fells in the Lakes. The views from Latrigg extend all the way over Derwent Water and into Borrowdale – the more popular one, not the peaceful one in route 13. The final part takes you into Fitz Park, a northern Lake District staple when it comes to green spaces within our towns and villages. The park has a pump track and gives you views over to Skiddaw and Latrigg.

It really is a mixed bag this one with some good multi-recreational routes, hard-packed gravel, singletrack and bridleways.

This ride really gives a true representation of what gravel riding is like in the northern part of the Lakes. There isn't anywhere to refuel or grab a brew after you make your way out of Threlkeld so ensure you have enough food and water with you.

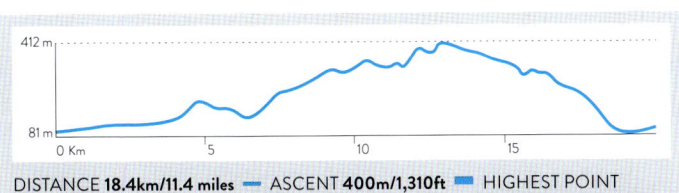

DISTANCE **18.4km/11.4 miles** — ASCENT **400m/1,310ft** — HIGHEST POINT **412m/1,350ft** — START/FINISH **Keswick** — START/FINISH GRID REF **NY 268234** — GPS **54.6012, -3.1346** — GRADE ■ — TERRAIN **Gravel; road; unpaved road; singletrack** — PARKING **Various options in Keswick** — MAP **OS Landranger 90, Penrith & Keswick (1:50,000)**

1 SKIDDAW IN EARLY SPRING. **2** VIEWS OF KESWICK FROM LATRIGG.

07 GLENDERATERRA

41

Directions

S Head north out of Keswick, crossing the River Greta on Station Road. Where the road curves to the right, go **SA** on to a cycle path (NCN route 71). Bear **R** to join the old railway line heading out towards the mountains.

2 Continue for around 3.5km until you reach a gate on the left shortly before a shelter on the right and a bridge.* If you fancy the challenge of another climb to reach Threlkeld, turn **L** and go through the gate. Go through another gate and turn **R** on to a lane. Climb up to reach the road at Wescoe then turn **R**; enjoy the flowing descent down to a junction on the edge of Threlkeld. Turn **L** to reach the centre of the village.

> **OR** *Alternatively, for a nice steady route to Threlkeld, continue **SA** along the railway line until you reach the A66. Turn **L**, following NCN route 71 alongside the A66. After 200m turn **L**, staying with NCN route 71 to reach the centre of Threlkeld.

3 Turn **L** in the village, signposted *Blease Road leading to Blencathra*. Climb (occasionally steeply) up the hill passing quaint Cumbria cottages and a radio tower – this is the last bit of tarmac you'll be seeing for a while. Continue until you reach the gate for the Blencathra Field Centre.

3 LOOKING ACROSS TO LONSCALE FELL.

4 Bear **R** here, staying on the road, which soon becomes gravel. There's more climbing to do as you contour around Blease Fell – all of a sudden you are in the middle of the mountains. There are some nice undulating sections here and a couple of beck crossings to negotiate. Cross a bridge and tackle a stiff climb to reach a path junction with the Cumbria Way.

5 Turn **L** along the Cumbria Way. Be warned – this part doesn't look like much of a cycling route. Prepare for a little hike-a-bike as you keep climbing up to the highest point of this route. There's some great flowing singletrack here as you descend around the side of Lonscale Fell. There are a couple of slab sections too. After crossing the slabs, the descent towards Latrigg steepens up. Follow the fence line all the way down then continue **SA** to cross Whit Beck; there are stunning views over towards Helvellyn and St John's in the Vale. Keep **L** after the beck to reach a road end under Latrigg.

6 Turn **R** on the road and go **L** through a gate after about 50m. Follow this bridleway (the Cumbria Way) down the hill and continue around a couple of zigzags. There are some technical sections and some drainage ditches to watch out for, so it's not as fast as the previous descent. Continue **SA** over the A66 to reach a road. Turn **R** along the road then shortly afterwards turn **L** through a gate into Fitz Park. Follow the path through the park, stopping for a few laps of the pump track if you feel like it, then turn **R** on to Station Road to return to your starting point.

■ 07 GLENDERATERRA

NEWLANDS VALLEY.

08 KESWICK & THE NEWLANDS VALLEY

23.9km/14.9 miles

Introduction

This route – which lies between the Newlands and Coledale horseshoes – is perfect for a warm summer's evening when nothing but a good ride is on the cards. Endless mountains, long flowing valleys and bubbling becks – this ride has it all. I particularly like this route because I've spent quite a bit of time hiking out here as well as on the bike, and I know it can feel miles away from civilisation.

The Cumbria Way and quiet roads take you out of Keswick, before a stint on the cycle path alongside the A66 takes you into the picturesque village of Braithwaite. Minor roads weave south through the Newlands Valley before you embark on a gravel out-and-back taking in the abandoned mines and waterfalls in the upper part of the valley. Don't skip this out-and-back, as the views and sense of adventure provided by this remote valley, along with the seeing some of history of the area, more than make up for having to retrace your steps.

Heading north again, the blast down the side of Cat Bells is a bridleway, but it feels more like a gnarly MTB descent; proceed with caution should you not feel confident on this type of terrain. Quiet lanes past the Lingholm Estate on the western shore of Derwent Water (a great food and coffee stop), lead back into bustling Keswick.

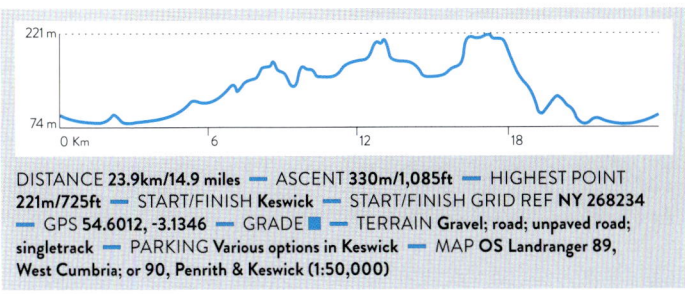

DISTANCE **23.9km/14.9 miles** — ASCENT **330m/1,085ft** — HIGHEST POINT **221m/725ft** — START/FINISH **Keswick** — START/FINISH GRID REF **NY 268234** — GPS **54.6012, -3.1346** — GRADE ■ — TERRAIN **Gravel; road; unpaved road; singletrack** — PARKING **Various options in Keswick** — MAP **OS Landranger 89, West Cumbria; or 90, Penrith & Keswick (1:50,000)**

1 ROUGH TRAIL UNDER HIGH SPY.

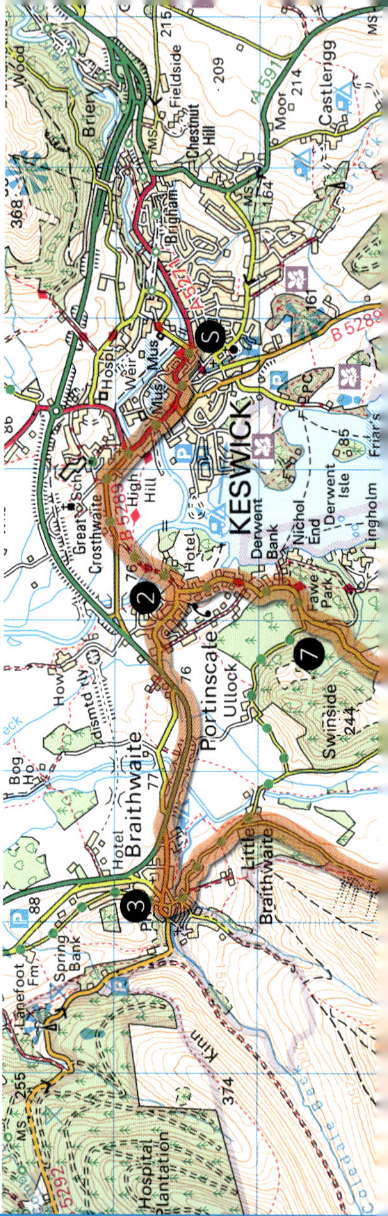

GRAVEL RIDES LAKE DISTRICT

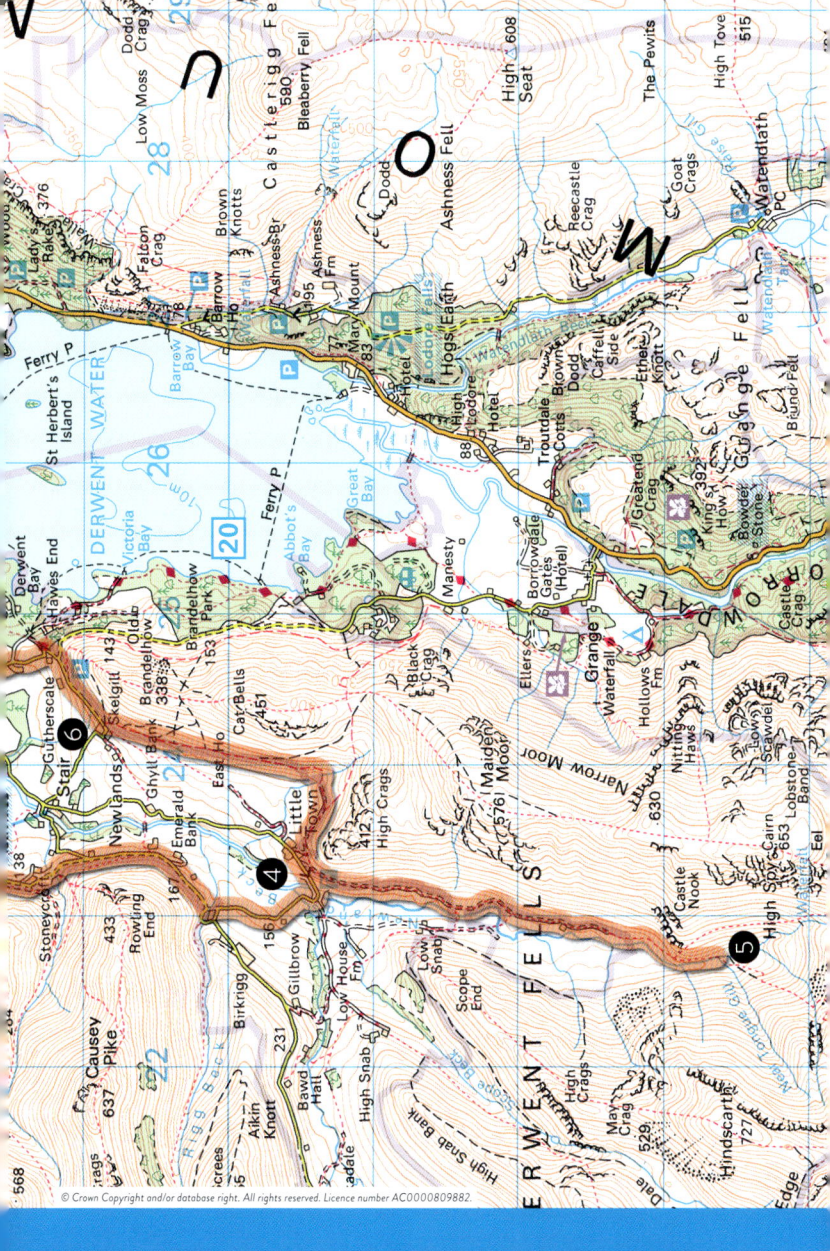

2 VIEW TOWARDS ROBINSON. © JOHN COEFIELD. **3** DALE HEAD AND WATERFALLS.

Directions

S Head west out of Keswick on the A5271. Cross the River Greta and keep left on the B5289 (also NCN route 71). After a few hundred metres turn **L** at a junction signed as a dead end road (still following NCN route 71) then dismount to cross an iron bridge over the River Derwent. Go **SA** on to a road and continue on, passing the Derwentwater Hotel, to reach a junction in Portinscale.

2 Turn **R**, following the signpost for *Keswick* and *Cockermouth*. Pass the Farmers Arms then turn **L** on to a cycle path which runs alongside the A66 (following the signpost for *Workington*, *Cockermouth* and *Braithwaite*). Follow the cycle path round to the **L** then follow the B5292 into Braithwaite. Continue **SA** through the village passing the Royal Oak.

3 Turn **L** immediately after the pub then cross a bridge over Coledale Beck; continue **SA** to start the climb to the Newlands Valley, following the signpost for *Newlands* and *Buttermere*. This quiet road climb is a treat – take in the stunning views of the Newlands Valley as you go; cross a cattle grid and keep climbing. At the top, the road curves sharply round to the right as it passes a footbridge; turn **L** shortly after this (following the signpost for *Newlands Ch.* and *Little Town* and passing a house with a purple door). Enjoy a lovely sweeping descent, cross two bridges then climb steeply.

Coffee and food
Fellpack, Lake Road Brunch, The Square Orange or Cafe West, Keswick; The Lingholm Kitchen, Lingholm Estate.

Bike shops
Biketreks, Keswick.

4 Just before a house on the right, turn **R** on to a track (going back on yourself) then go through a metal gate. This is the start of an out-and-back gravel section, passing some abandoned mines and magnificent waterfalls. The track is a little bit lumpy in places. Continue past the Carlisle Mountaineering Club hut (where the track dissipates and turns into singletrack in places) to reach a waterfall at the end.

5 Retrace your steps to reach the road again. Turn **R** on to the road and shortly afterwards turn **R** on to a bridleway. Keep **L** to stay on the bridleway (following the signpost for *Hause Gate*) – continue on this steep, gravelly climb to reach a junction. Turn **L** at the junction. Cross a bridge then turn **L** again, passing some little cairns. Keep these on your left-hand side and continue **SA** on to a singletrack bridleway, which runs next to a drystone wall. This descent underneath Cat Bells is fast (and a little technical in a few places), with some slabs and lumpy parts; continue on, going through a yellow barrier, to reach a narrow road in Skelgill.

6 Turn **R** on to the road then turn **L** at the next junction, following the signposts for *Portinscale* and *Keswick*. After about 2km you'll pass the entrance to the Lingholm Estate on your right.

7 Shortly afterwards, a lane (also NCN route 71) joins from the left. Continue along the road to reach Portinscale. Turn **R** in the village (following the blue NCN route 71/C2C cycling sign) and retrace your outward route back into Keswick.

■ **08 KESWICK & THE NEWLANDS VALLEY**

DESCENT TO LANGDALE FROM BLEA TARN.

09 **TILBERTHWAITE & LANGDALE**
25.2km/15.7 miles

Introduction

This route arguably takes in some of the most stunning landscapes you'll find in the Lakes. Starting to the north of Coniston Water in Tilberthwaite, the first section takes you through peaceful woodland to Little Langdale. Abandoned quarries dot the landscape, hinting at a very different history to what is visible now.

A stiff climb up to Blea Tarn, which sits in a small hanging valley, will test your legs. While you catch your breath at the top you can make the most of the view towards the Langdale Pikes. This tarn was one of the first that I visited when I started falling in love with the Lake District. The descent into Great Langdale is fast and fun, which is followed by a relaxed section by the river, before another tough climb over the flanks of Lingmoor Fell.

If you need some refreshment at this point in the ride, the Three Shires Inn is a good option. Named after the nearby Three Shire Stone, it marks where the historic counties of Westmorland, Lancashire and Cumberland met. More riverside trails and forests then take you back to Tilberthwaite.

There's a good variety of terrain throughout this ride, mostly either minor roads or what I'd class as prime gravel, so you can keep the hammer down if you consider yourself a hitter or alternatively cruise along and take in the scenery. I generally prefer the latter.

All in all, this is one of my favourite routes in this book – it has a bit of everything and, better still, despite the climbs, its rideable for almost anyone at any level. Remember its perfectly okay to get off and push your bike if you have to!

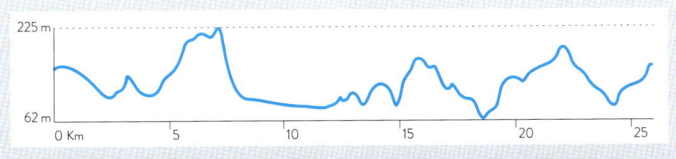

DISTANCE **25.2km/15.7 miles** — ASCENT **480m/1,575ft** — HIGHEST POINT **225m/740ft** — START/FINISH **Tilberthwaite** — START/FINISH GRID REF **NY 306009** — GPS **54.3997, -3.0699** — GRADE ■ — TERRAIN **Gravel; road; unpaved road; rough track** — PUBLIC TRANSPORT **Bus to nearby Ambleside** — PARKING **Tilberthwaite car park (parking charge)** — MAP **OS Landranger 90, Penrith & Keswick; 96, Barrow-in-Furness & South Lakeland (1:50,000)**

1 LITTLE LANGDALE TARN. **2** HEADING UP BLEA TARN PASS.
3 DESCENT FROM THE 'CHALLENGING OPTION'.

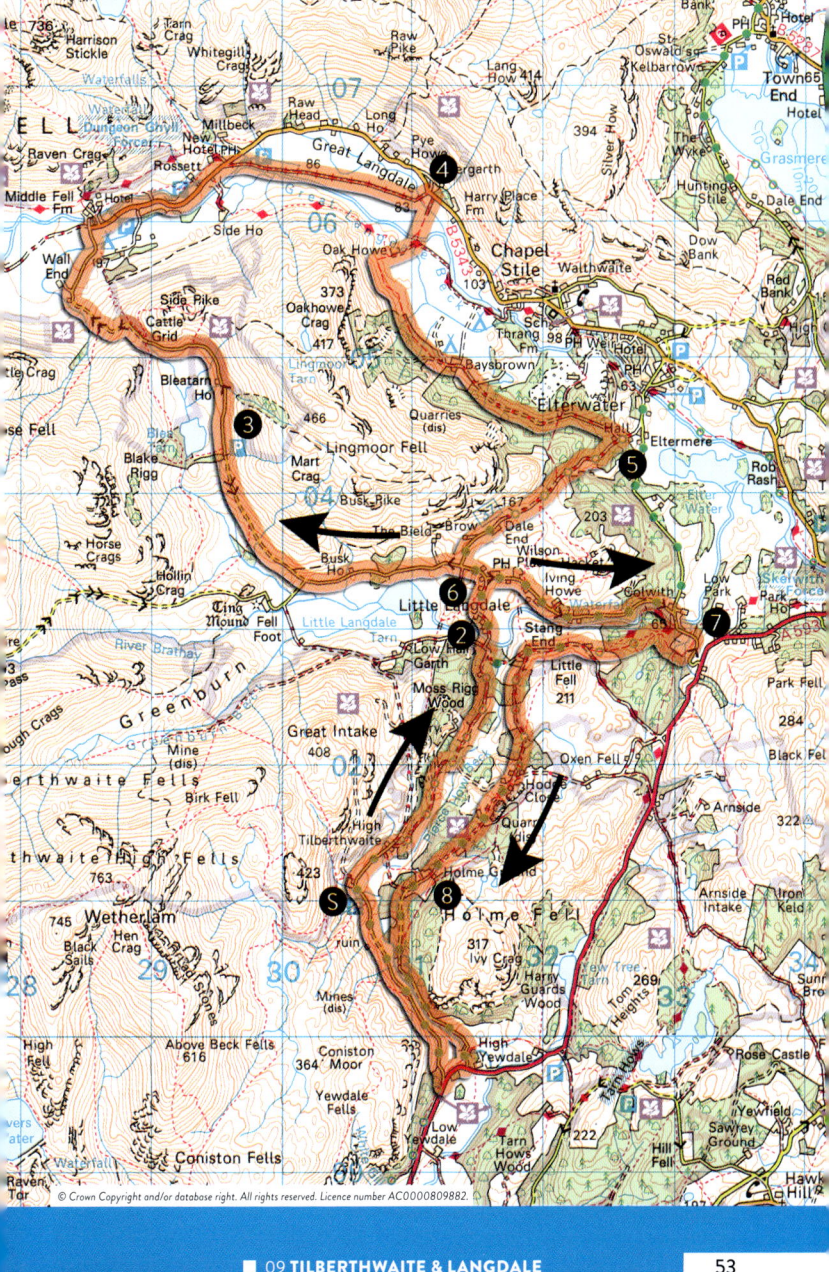

09 TILBERTHWAITE & LANGDALE

Directions

S Head north from Low Tilberthwaite following NCN route 637 along a minor road. Turn **R** at High Tilberthwaite (still following NCN route 637) along the smooth, undulating gravel bridleway that connects Tilberthwaite with Little Langdale. Bear **L** to reach a bridge over the River Brathay. (Just around the corner to the left of the bridge is Cathedral Quarry. The Cathedral itself is a 12-metre-tall cavern that was mined out for slate with a central gigantic pillar holding the roof up – rather impressive and worth a quick stop.)

2 Cross the bridge and go **SA** along the singletrack lane known as Fitz Steps; this will bring you out on Side Gates (to your right you'll be able to see the Three Shires Inn). Turn **L** along the road (take care in peak season as this road can become busy). Looking over to your left you'll see Little Langdale Tarn, with Great Intake, Birk Fell and Wetherlam standing tall and creating a stunning backdrop. Follow the road and descend for just over 1km, cross a cattle grid then fork **R**, following the signpost for *Blea Tarn* and *Great Langdale*. Initially the climb starts off at a moderate percentage, but it does ramp up to 25%; continue on to reach Blea Tarn.

3 Keep going on the road past the tarn. The descent into Great Langdale is super fun and super steep with an abundance of switchbacks, so keep those brakes covered and look out for sheep and potholes. This road becomes the B5343 at the valley floor; follow the road for just over 1km then, just before the turning for the New Dungeon Ghyll Hotel, turn **R** on to a byway, following the signpost for *Elterwater* and *Ambleside*. This gravel track cuts across the valley floor to meet the B5343 again.

Coffee and food
The Green Housekeeper, Coniston; Lanty Slee's, Great Langdale; Three Shires Inn, Little Langdale; Chesters by the River, Skelwith Bridge; Britannia Inn, Elterwater.

Bike shops
Ghyllside Cycles or Push Cartel, Ambleside.

4 GOOD GRAVEL THROUGH THE HEART OF GREAT LANGDALE. **5** BRIDGE OVER THE RIVER BRATHAY.

❹ Just before the B5343 (immediately after crossing a beck and before the track climbs to the road), a trail heads off **R** – take this. Turn **R** again after 100m on to another bridleway. Cross the bridge and turn **R** towards some buildings at Oak Howe, then keep **L** after the buildings to follow the bridleway as it heads south-east towards Baysbrown. Continue **SA** through Baysbrown towards Elterwater Hall.

❺ Turn sharp **R** just before the hall. (Alternatively you can descend to the lane into Elterwater if you'd like to visit the Britannia Inn.) This long and lumpy ascent takes you back over Lingmoor Fell, then descends and turns into a singletrack lane just after a farm to meet the road in Little Langdale again.

❻ Turn **L** and follow the road to Colwith then turn **R**, following the signpost for *Ambleside* and *Coniston*.

❼ Cross the river then after 150m turn **R** on to a bridleway following the signpost for *NCN route 637* and *Coniston*. Keep **R** then turn **L**, joining NCN route 637 to reach Stang End. Turn **L** on to a byway (still following NCN route 637) underneath Holme Fell and passing Hodge Close Quarry.

❽ The byway turns into a minor road at Holme Ground. Continue along the road then, just before reaching the A593, turn **R** on to a bridleway. Follow this alongside the A593 for a short distance then turn **R**, following the signpost for *Tilberthwaite*, to return to the start.

■ 09 **TILBERTHWAITE & LANGDALE**

DESCENT NEAR TARN HOWS.

10 GRIZEDALE FOREST

38km/23.6 miles

Introduction

Grizedale is the Mecca for gravel riding in the South Lakes with its 24 square kilometres of forest filled with prime fire roads. Situated between Windermere and Coniston Water, no matter which part of the forest you're riding in you'll see jaw-dropping vistas. What I like about riding here the most is that I feel completely cut off from the rest of the Lakes. If you're wanting to escape the hustle and bustle of the national park, this is the way to do it.

Starting south of Satterthwaite, forest roads and trails take you past Grizedale Tarn, a small body of water nestled between the pine trees. Often a tranquil spot, I have found myself on numerous occasions staying here way longer than I anticipated, watching the abundance of dragonflies in the summer months. More trails take you north to the Coppermines Valley, which offers a great contrast to the forest, and on to Coniston. Next there is a peaceful section of road along the eastern shore of Coniston Water, a decent spot for a swim if you fancy it, before forest tracks take you back to your start point.

I ride in here on a regular basis and I'm always finding a new vantage point or a new gravel trail to try. This really is Lakes gravel at its best; if you're less experienced at riding on technical terrain and want the ground underneath your tyres to be as primo as possible then this is absolutely the route for you. Having said that, this ride isn't to be underestimated – there's a lot of climbing in a relatively short distance but it's totally worth it, like it always is.

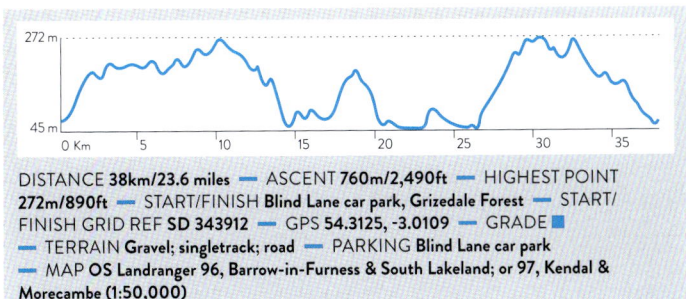

DISTANCE **38km/23.6 miles** — ASCENT **760m/2,490ft** — HIGHEST POINT **272m/890ft** — START/FINISH **Blind Lane car park, Grizedale Forest** — START/FINISH GRID REF **SD 343912** — GPS **54.3125, -3.0109** — GRADE ■ — TERRAIN **Gravel; singletrack; road** — PARKING **Blind Lane car park** — MAP **OS Landranger 96, Barrow-in-Furness & South Lakeland; or 97, Kendal & Morecambe (1:50,000)**

1 DROPPING INTO THE SINGLETRACK. **2** SMILE FOR THE CAMERA, NICK. LOG PILE PHOTOS ARE ALWAYS A MUST!

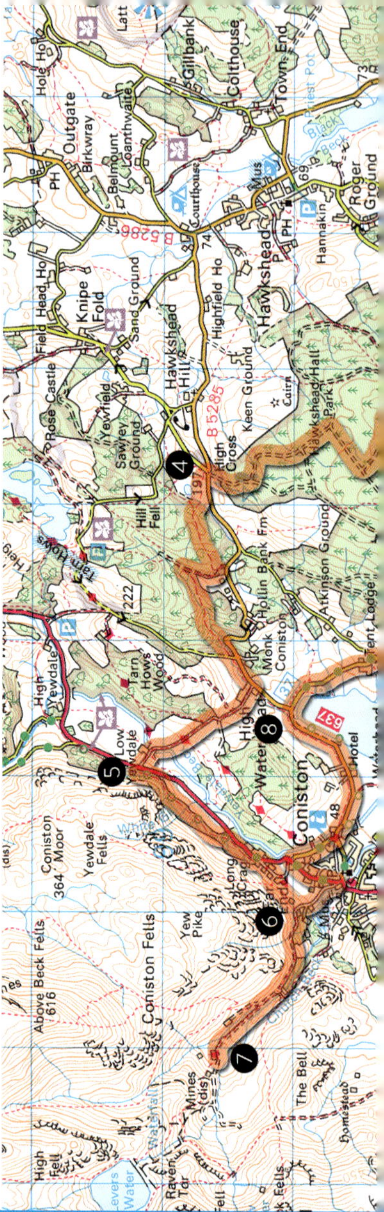

GRAVEL RIDES LAKE DISTRICT

10 GRIZEDALE FOREST

3 PRIME GRIZEDALE GRAVEL. **4** CONISTON WATER AND THE CONISTON FELLS.

Directions

S Turn **L** out of the car park and on to the road, heading north-east. After 250m turn **L** to start a fairly hefty winch up a fire road. As you gain height, you can look over the South Lakes peninsulas – on a clear day you can make out the Hoad Monument near Ulverston. Go **SA** at a junction to reach Grizedale Tarn.

2 Retrace your steps from the tarn to reach the junction; turn **L** here on to a short descent then bear **L**. The track levels out for a while; turn **R** for a slightly longer descent and continue **SA** to meet the road at Moor Top.

3 Turn **R** then almost immediately turn **L** into Moor Top car park. Continue through the car park; this part of the route makes its way through the forest, generally heading north, to High Cross. Stick to the GPX or pay close attention to the map here, as there are loads of trails in the forest. The route undulates for a time, before descending (make the most of the views here) to reach the road at High Cross.

4 Go **SA** on to a prime gravel track; this is a super-smooth, fast and fun descent but watch out for walkers. Again, keep an eye on the GPX and map here, as there are quite a few turnings. This eventually runs alongside, then meets, the B5285. Turn **R** on to the road then immediately turn **R** on to a track. This crosses Yewdale Beck to meet the A593.

5 Cross the road and go **SA** on to a trail which leads to NCN route 637. Turn **L**, heading towards Coniston. This is super smooth, but can be a little overgrown in the summer months. There are a few becks to cross – err on the side of caution because these can become relatively deep when in spate, and the woodwork on the bridges also becomes slippery when wet. Continue on until you reach a junction.

Coffee and food
The Green Housekeeper, Coniston; Cafe Ambio, Grizedale Forest visitor centre.

Bike shops
Biketreks, Grizedale Forest.

6 Turn **R**, heading up into the Coppermines Valley. (You can miss out this out-and-back section by turning left and going into Coniston.) This is a gradual climb before it plateaus to reach the YHA hostel – a good place to stay.

7 Retrace your steps (the descent is quite fast) to the junction at **6**; keep **R** here to reach the A593 (detouring into Coniston to refuel if needed). Turn **L** on to the A593 then turn **R**, following the signpost for *Hawkshead*, *The Lake* and *Tarn Hows*. Turn **L** on to the B5285 then bear **L** on to NCN route 637, which runs alongside the road.

8 As the road curves to the left, leave the cycle path and turn **R**, following the signpost for *Monk Coniston*. Pass Monk Coniston car park and continue on this generally quiet road, which heads due south and undulates along the shore of Coniston Water. There are a few spots where you can get down to the water should you want a mid-ride swim.

9 Around 4km after the car park, turn **L** on to a track next to a couple of houses (the turning isn't marked and it's fairly nondescript) and start the climb back up to Grizedale. This monster climb can feel like it goes on forever, but the views are ample reward for your efforts. Again, keep an eye on the GPX and map in the forest, as there are quite a few turnings. Follow the zigzags up the hill to reach a bridleway at the top.

10 It's practically all downhill from here. Turn **R** on to the bridleway, then take the second **R** turn on to a track. Enjoy the super flowing, fast descent all the way down to a road south of Satterthwaite. Turn **R** along the road then turn **L** to return to the start.

SHORESIDE GRAVEL.

11 STAVELEY TO SHORESIDE

48km/29.8 miles

Introduction

This ride takes in some of the classic South Lakes gravel. It really has it all from super-smooth, flowing singletrack along the shores of Windermere to slate slabs to descend over where picking your line is everything, testing your confidence and ability. Crossing over three different valleys with some extremely picturesque views, this is almost as good as it gets for the South Lakes. Overall, this is a well-balanced ride and can be enjoyed by almost everyone because, even on the rough stuff, there's always the option to get off and push should you feel out of your depth.

Starting in Staveley, the ride utilises a mixture of bridleways, byways and minor roads to cross over into Troutbeck. Next there is more climbing followed by a fun descent through Jenkin Crag down into picturesque Ambleside. A loop under Loughrigg Fell takes you round to the western shore of Windermere, where there's some nice relaxed riding alongside the water. A quick ferry ride takes you across Windermere before more quiet lanes and bridleways deliver you back to Staveley. Despite being a small village there's an abundance of everything in Staveley – cafes, bakeries, coffee shops and, most importantly, a bike shop.

To summarise this ride, it has all the key elements we want from a gravel ride: premium gravel, some singletrack, doubletrack, the lumpy stuff and testing slabs. The inevitable connecting sections or road do not detract from the good stuff – this is a great day out. There are places to eat and drink along the way, but this ride will also give you a wild and remote feeling, something that the Lakes is well and truly competent at.

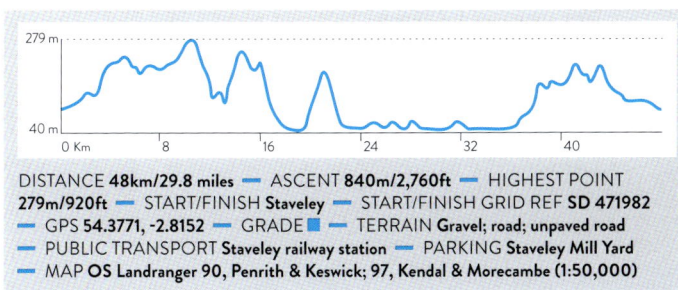

DISTANCE **48km/29.8 miles** — ASCENT **840m/2,760ft** — HIGHEST POINT **279m/920ft** — START/FINISH **Staveley** — START/FINISH GRID REF **SD 471982** — GPS **54.3771, -2.8152** — GRADE ■ — TERRAIN **Gravel; road; unpaved road** — PUBLIC TRANSPORT **Staveley railway station** — PARKING **Staveley Mill Yard** — MAP **OS Landranger 90, Penrith & Keswick; 97, Kendal & Morecambe (1:50,000)**

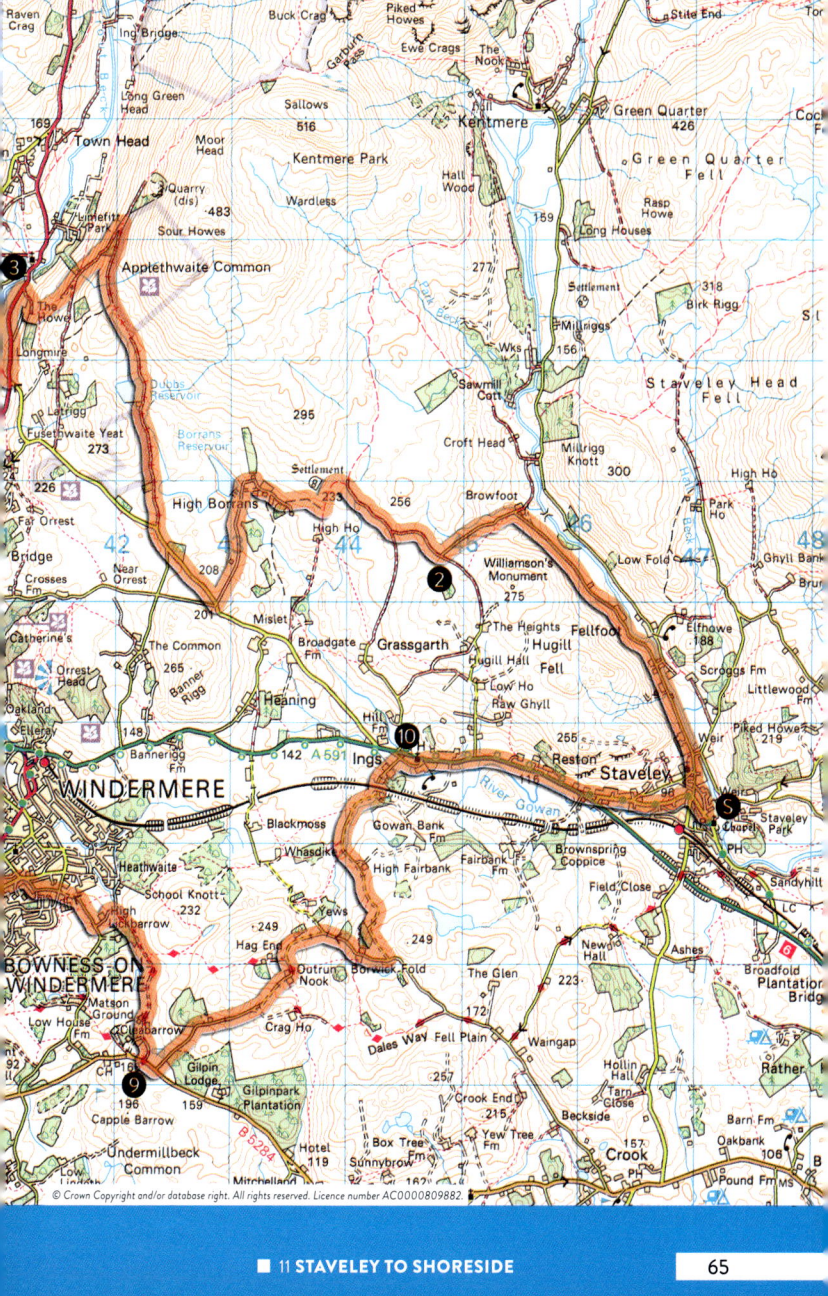

11 STAVELEY TO SHORESIDE

65

Directions

S Starting out from Staveley Mill Yard turn **R** on to Back Lane then **R** again on to Silver Street, which runs alongside the River Kent for a short while. Continue **SA** on to Browfoot Lane. This is a dead end, so it's relatively traffic free – enjoy soaking up the scenery of the surrounding fells.

2 Once at the top of Kentmere, turn **R** (heading west) on to a bridleway towards Borrans Reservoir – this is where the good gravel begins. Keep **SA** at the next two junctions then turn **R** before High House. Follow Borrans Lane past Borrans Reservoir to meet tarmac again. Turn **R** then take the first **R** on to a byway (Dubbs Road), passing Dubbs Reservoir. Turn **L** above the caravan park at Limefitt for your first proper descent, down into Troutbeck. This is mostly good gravel, however there can be deep ruts along with some really chunky stuff. Keep the reins in and look out for walkers, as this descent meets the Garburn Pass which is popular with walkers heading for the Kentmere Horseshoe. Continue on to reach the A592.

3 Turn **L** for a short, flat section on the A592 then turn **R** for a punchy climb on a usually overgrown bridleway that pops you out in Town End. Go **SA** on to a short section of bridleway, turn **L** along a minor road then turn **R** on to a bridleway. Turn **L** to begin the hellish climb on Robin Lane; in this instance the effort is well worth the reward as the bridleway soon opens up to give you a real Lakeland feel and stunning views right down Windermere.

4 Here's where the further fun begins; I really enjoy this part of the ride. Starting your descent towards Ambleside, heading along High Skelghyll, you find yourself skirting alongside the flanks of Wansfell Pike before heading into Jenkin Crag, a remarkable woodland high up on the fell. Caution is advised when riding through here – there are some great big features which are all rideable, but they can be very slippery when wet, which is most of the year. The bridleway becomes a road (Skelghyll Lane). Turn **L** on to Old Lake Road to reach the A591 on the outskirts of Ambleside.

5 To bypass the village, turn **L** on the the A591 then turn **R** on to MacIver Lane, **R** on to the A5075, then turn **L** on to the A593, crossing the River Rothay. (Alternatively, detour into Ambleside to take in this tourist hotspot – abundant with shops, cafes and galleries, there's plenty to see should you want to give yourself an hour or two before the second leg of the ride.) Just after crossing the river turn **R** on to a minor road (Under Loughrigg) following NCN route 6 alongside the River Rothay. Go over a cattle grid then turn **L** on to a bridleway under Loughrigg Fell. Climb and then descend west over Loughrigg Fell, keeping to the bridleway. As the descent swings right by a wall, turn **L** to reach a minor road at Brunt How. Turn **L** and then **L** again on to the A593.

1 BRIDLEWAY TO WINDERMERE.

Coffee and food
Mr Duffins Coffee or More?, Staveley; Copper Pot or The Apple Pie, Ambleside; Homeground, Windermere.

Bike shops
Wheelbase, Staveley; Biketreks, Ings; Ghyllside Cycles or Push Cartel, Ambleside.

6 Turn **R** on to a path to cross the River Brathay via a stone bridge then turn **L**. Turn **R** at the junction to rejoin NCN route 6 which runs alongside the B5286, heading south. The NCN trail crosses from one side of the road to the other a few times and occasionally joins the road for short sections. Just keep following the blue NCN route 6 signs. Be sure to follow the signed trail just after the entrance to Wray Castle, not the castle drive itself. This trail leads down to the Windermere shoreside and the NCN route runs southwards from here on the western side of the lake. This section of the route is plain sailing as its mostly flat.

7 Weave your way along to the Windermere Ferry. This takes bikes for a small charge; the crossing takes a mere 10 minutes and before you know it you are dropped into the hustle and bustle of Bowness-on-Windermere.

8 The punchy climb out of Bowness follows NCN route 6 and eventually on to the A5074 before turning **R** on to Thornbarrow Road; you'll very much have to find your legs again for this one as it can become quite a pull up. Turn **R** on to Lickbarrow Road; after you leave the houses behind turn **L** on to a minor road marked by a signpost for a *Gated single track road*. Turn **R** on to a byway underneath School Knott (there's a small tarn just off the track; the summit isn't much further either and it's well worth a walk on the footpath up to the top for panoramic views as far as the Old Man of Coniston to the west and Kentmere Pike to the east) to reach a road.

9 Turn **L** and immediately **L** again on a minor road heading towards Ings. This section takes in what is known locally as 'the gated road' – as you might expect there are many, many gates. This part of the route is rather undulating so opening and closing the gates can provide a welcome breather. Turn **L** after Borwick Fold over a cattle grid following the blue cycle route signs then turn **R** just before Ings to reach the A591.

10 Turn **R** on to NCN route 6 alongside the A591. Continue following NCN route 6 as it leaves the A591 and turns **L** along Danes Road into Staveley. Turn **L** on to Back Lane to return to Staveley Mill Yard.

■ **11 STAVELEY TO SHORESIDE**

WHINFELL – THE DEAD-END ROAD (ROUTE 13)

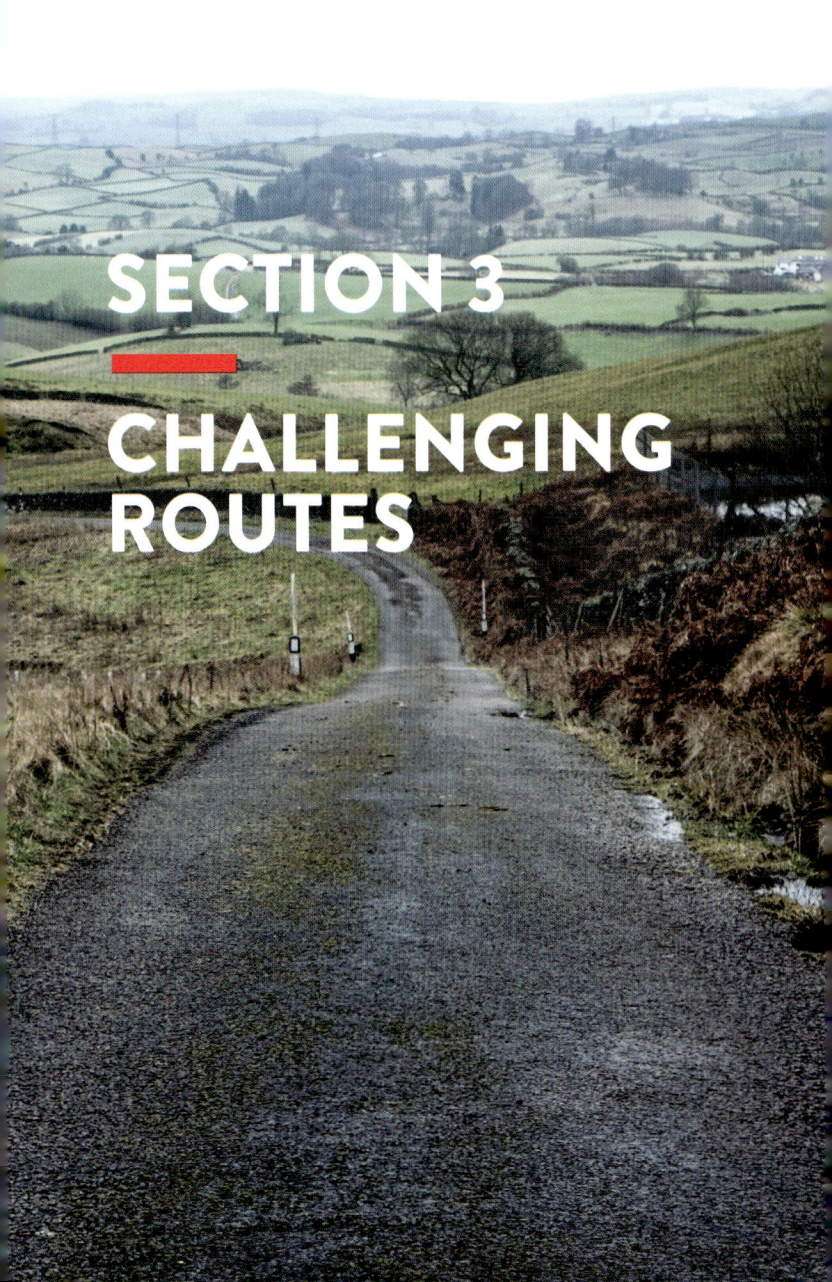

SECTION 3
CHALLENGING ROUTES

KENTMERE COMMON.

12 **KENTMERE**

17km/10.6 miles

Introduction

Kentmere is usually known as 'Gatemere' among us locals; however, the abundance of gates provides us with a great excuse to slow down and truly take in this exceptionally stunning valley. There is evidence to show that the Kentmere Valley was first inhabited around 6,000 years ago (look out for an old settlement as you descend towards Long Houses). Today, the valley is sparsely populated; you'll generally only see locals and farm traffic.

The ride starts in Staveley before climbing on some minor roads then byways and bridleways along the eastern flank of the valley. Kentmere village is tiny but has the picturesque St Cuthbert's Church and the frankly spooky Kentmere Hall. I always wonder at this point how far I'd get on my gravel bike going further up the valley towards the tempting views of Kentmere Pike before I had to get off and walk. I'm pretty confident I know the answer to my own question, but luckily there's plenty to be ridden within the valley.

Moving on past Kentmere there is a climb on a rough and sometimes technical bridleway underneath Kentmere Park. The descent down to Ings is speedy and fun, before a stint on a cycle path rolls you back to Staveley for coffee.

Something to be aware of is that Kentmere is exceptionally wet all year round. I strongly recommend doing this route in the drier months of the year. Don't be put off (I have done this route in wet weather), but it can be a bit soggy over the tops. To conclude, Kentmere is yet another quiet corner of the Lakes that is almost completely unknown to the general public, but is a location where locals seek solitude and soggy feet alike.

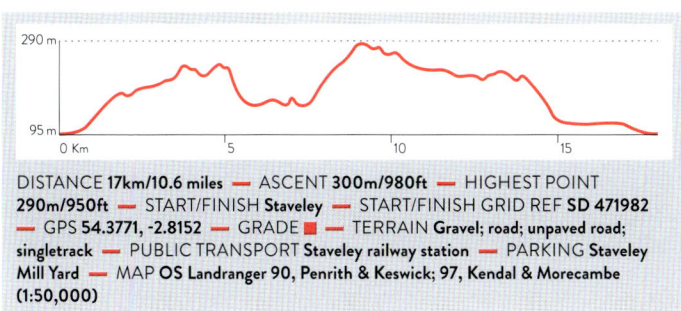

DISTANCE **17km/10.6 miles** — ASCENT **300m/980ft** — HIGHEST POINT **290m/950ft** — START/FINISH **Staveley** — START/FINISH GRID REF **SD 471982** — GPS **54.3771, -2.8152** — GRADE ■ — TERRAIN **Gravel; road; unpaved road; singletrack** — PUBLIC TRANSPORT **Staveley railway station** — PARKING **Staveley Mill Yard** — MAP **OS Landranger 90, Penrith & Keswick; 97, Kendal & Morecambe (1:50,000)**

1 SUNSET OVER APPLETHWAITE COMMON.

12 KENTMERE

Directions

S Starting out from Staveley Mill Yard turn **R** on to Back Lane then **R** again on to Silver Street, which runs alongside the River Kent. Turn **R** over the bridge (signposted *Burneside*). Keep **L** after the bridge; this road climb on Hall Lane is prolonged and progressive, so it'll get your legs well and truly warmed up as you skirt up and along the north-east flank of the valley. This dead-end road doesn't see much traffic; it turns into a good gravel byway at Park House so you'll feel right at home before you know it.

2 After around 700m on the byway turn **L** on to a bridleway; continue **SA** at the next junction heading north-west across the fell and descending into the valley. This part of the ride across the open fellside is great; in the spring these hills are abundant with young livestock so do make sure you close the gates behind you. Be aware that there are a couple of becks to cross on the descent and it is lumpy and bumpy and has slippery rocks in places – it is all rideable but take your time. Look out for the old settlement on your left as you descend towards the road at Long Houses.

3 Turn **R** on to the road. Keep **L** (following the signpost for *Kentmere Church*) then cross a bridge to head into the village. Bear **L** on to a gravel bridleway opposite St Cuthbert's Church. A short distance after the church you'll pass Kentmere Hall,

Coffee and food
Mr Duffins Coffee, More? or Wilf's Cafe, Staveley.

Bike shops
Wheelbase, Staveley; Biketreks, Ings.

2 ASCENT IN THE KENTMERE VALLEY.
3 ADAM ENJOYING THE VIEW.
4 TAKING A WELL-EARNED BREATHER.

a fourteenth-century tower house. After the hall there is a long gravel climb on a bridleway – it is rough and can be quite technical depending on recent weather. At the top the views open out to the south; on a good day you can see as far as Morecambe. Going across the tops here can be a little arduous in some instances; it's undulating, rough singletrack that's really rutted in places. Beware of pedal strikes and any deep puddles. I strongly advise taking your time here unless you're on a plus-sized gravel bike or hardtail mountain bike. Go **SA** at the next junction then continue on to reach a junction with a rough 4x4 track.

4 Turn **L** on to the track – your patience with the rough singletrack will be rewarded here as this track is fast and fun. Keep **R** at the next junction to reach the farm at Grassgarth. Go **SA** through the farm and continue along the minor road to reach the A591 at Ings.

5 Turn **L** on to the cycleway (NCN route 6) which runs alongside the A591, soon passing Biketreks on your right. Continue following NCN route 6 as it leaves the A591 and turns **L** along Danes Road into Staveley. Turn **L** on to Back Lane to return to Staveley Mill Yard.

■ 12 KENTMERE

HEADING ALONG THE BORROWDALE VALLEY.

13 THE OTHER BORROWDALE

31km/19.3 miles

Introduction

It's such a treat to be able to do this route straight from my own front door. A convenient start in Kendal soon delivers you to the wilderness of the 'other Borrowdale'. The more famous, and consequently busier, Borrowdale sits just south of Keswick. However, the other Borrowdale, which sits between Kendal and Shap, is equally jaw dropping but blissfully quiet.

From Kendal, quiet lanes follow the River Mint past Whinfell Tarn, heading north to the foot of Whinfell Beacon. The climb up to the beacon is tough, but the views across to the Howgills and to the Lake District fells are amazing. Now follows a fun and rocky descent into Borrowdale. The climb up the valley towards the A6 is gentle. A mix of byways and quiet roads around the farms and rural cottages of Garth Row and a stint on the A6 take you south and back to Kendal.

I'd consider this route to be relatively tough; if you are not ascending you are either riding in deep gravel or descending some pretty gnarly terrain. This ride is probably best done in the drier months of the year; waterproof socks or shoes are a wise precaution for the yomp over the fell if there has been recent rainfall. It's a route that requires a fair bit of patience and time. Don't be put off – the effort-versus-reward ratio is way, way up there. I encourage you to just go and ride this and you'll see exactly what I mean.

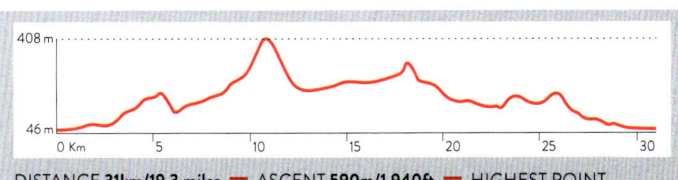

DISTANCE **31km/19.3 miles** — ASCENT **590m/1,940ft** — HIGHEST POINT **408m/1,340ft** — START/FINISH **Kendal railway station** — START/FINISH GRID REF **SD 519931** — GPS **54.3316, -2.7411** — ALTERNATIVE START **Lay-by on the A6 near Garth Row** — ALTERNATIVE START/FINISH GRID REF **SD 530969** — ALTERNATIVE GPS **54.3663, -2.7234** — GRADE ■ — TERRAIN **Hard-packed gravel; tarmac; rough bridleway; singletrack; deep gravel** — PUBLIC TRANSPORT **Bus and train connections to Kendal** — PARKING **Various options in Kendal or lay-by at alternative start point** — MAP **OS Landranger 90, Penrith & Keswick; 91, Appleby-in-Westmorland; 97, Kendal & Morecambe (1:50,000)**

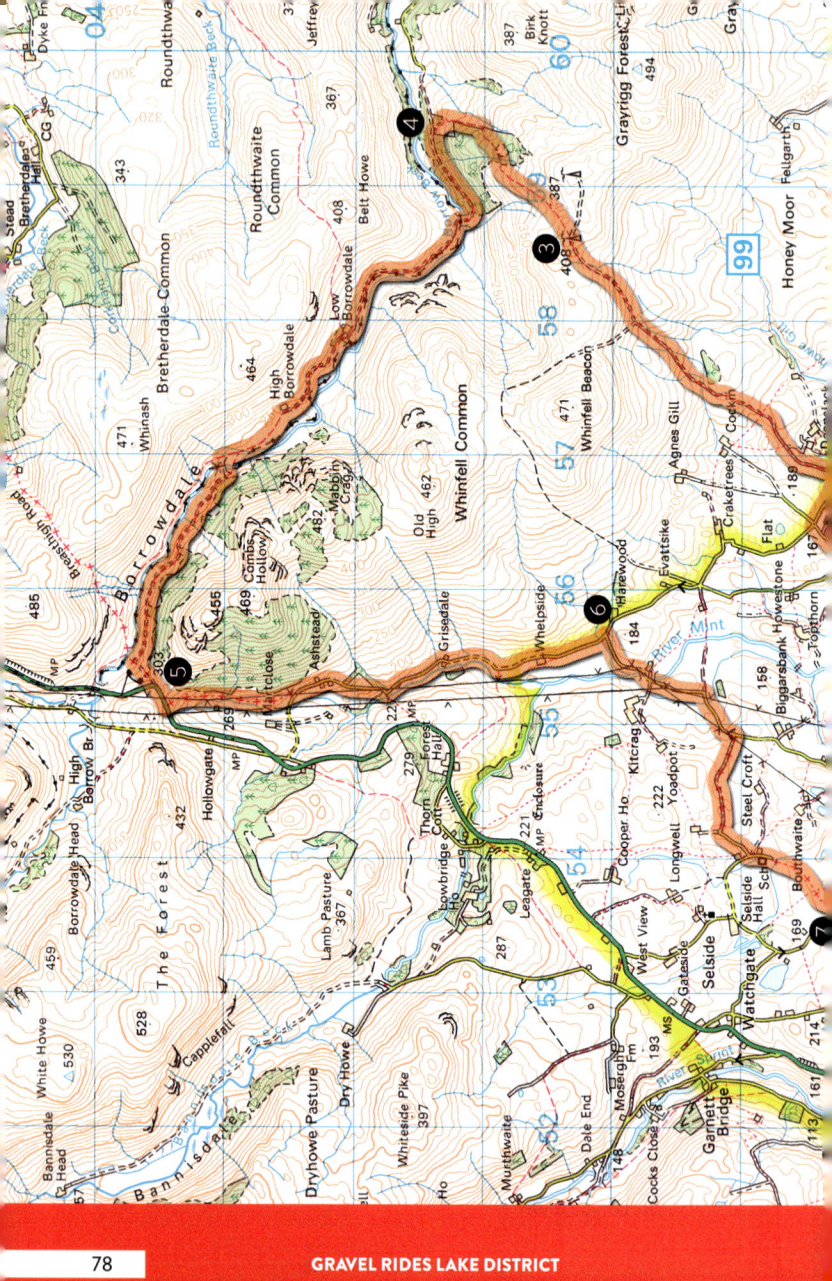

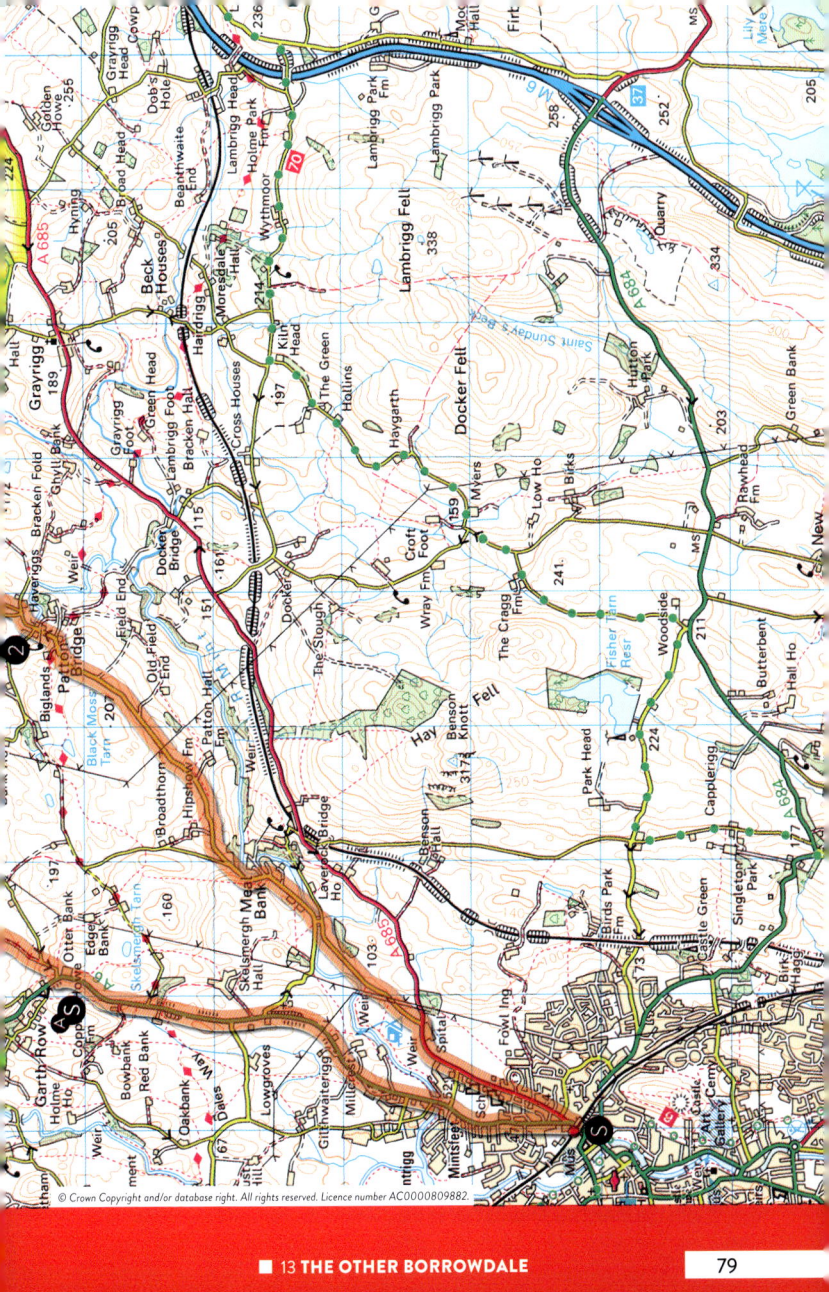

Directions

S Exit the station and turn **L** on to the A6; shortly afterwards bear **R** on to the A685. Leaving the town behind, pass a farm on the right then turn **L**, following the signpost for *Mealbank*, *Patton* and *Whinfell*. The road runs alongside the River Mint for a while then crosses the river on a lovely arched stone bridge. Continue on the road as it crosses the River Mint again at Patton Bridge.

2 Continue on this road as you start the main climb of the route towards Whinfell Beacon – this singletrack road is generally only used by the service vehicles for the beacon or by local farmers. The climb is tough and sustained but exceedingly rewarding. Pass Whinfell Tarn then bear **R**, following the signpost for *Grayrigg*. Turn **R** at the next junction, again following the signpost for *Grayrigg*. At a crossroads after 500m turn **L** and go through a gate on to a tarmac road; this road takes you all the way to the beacon at 408m. On a clear day the views are stunning, with the main Lake District fells to the west and the Howgill Fells to the east.

Coffee and food
Fold Coffee, Podda & Wren, The Bakery at No.4 or Marra, Kendal.

Bike shops
Brucie's Bike Shop or Giant, Kendal.

1 MINOR ROAD FROM MEAL BANK TO PATTON BRIDGE. **2** UP UP UP TO WHINFELL BEACON. **3** THE ROAD CLIMB TOWARDS WHINFELL. **4** VIEW INTO BORROWDALE.

③ Leaving the tarmac behind, continue **SA** from the beacon on to a path. Take care to stick to the GPX or pay close attention to the map here as you disappear over the top of the fell and start descending to the valley below. The top two thirds of the descent are rocky, rutted and boggy singletrack, turning into very rough doubletrack for the final third.

④ Turn **L** on to a bridleway at the bottom to start the gentle ascent through Borrowdale. The 5km ride along the valley is a treat. You start on the southern side of Borrow Beck on good doubletrack (although be aware there are plenty of potholes), then cross to the northern side to reach the farm at Low Borrowdale. As you make your way towards the farm at High Borrowdale the surface becomes predominantly grassy. You'll eventually cross over the beck again where the surface becomes gravel again. The gravel is deep in places here so ride with caution or just keep plodding along. The climb ramps up for the last short section before the A6.

⑤ Turn **L** on to the A6 then after 150m turn **L** and go through a gate on to a byway. At the end of the byway continue **SA** on to a minor road. Follow the road as it contours around the side of Whinfell Common and passes through a few farms to reach a junction at Harewood.

⑥ Turn **R** on to another minor road; this passes a house then crosses the River Mint. Around 1km after the river turn **R** on to a byway. Turn **L** at the end of the byway on to a minor road. Follow this for 250m then turn **L**; this minor road passes a farm on the left and a school on the right before turning into a byway. Follow this to reach a road.

⑦ Turn **L** on to the road then immediately turn **R** on to Dry Lane (a byway). At the end of the byway turn **R** on to a minor road; follow this for a short distance to reach the A6. Turn **L** on to the A6 and follow it back into Kendal.

■ 13 **THE OTHER BORROWDALE**

BLENCATHRA FROM THE OLD COACH ROAD. © JOHN COEFIELD.

14 SKIDDAW HOUSE & THE OLD COACH ROAD

57.3km/35.6 miles

Introduction

Out of all the routes in this book so far, I'd consider this one to be the most demanding. This is mainly due to the riding terrain – be prepared for rough and rocky tracks – it really takes no prisoners. On the flip side, this route has some of the most enjoyable sections of gravel riding the Lakes has to offer, along with truly sensational views and an unbeatable feeling of adventure.

Starting in Keswick, the first section takes you around the northern side of Latrigg before a climb into the Glenderaterra Valley and north on the Cumbria Way to Skiddaw House. This youth hostel is one of the most remote in the UK and makes a great stopover if you want to take your time and do this ride over two days. There is also a remote bothy north-west of the route providing another option for a microadventure.

From the hostel, a descent on rough gravel and then on tarmac brings you through the Caldew Valley to Mosedale. Next, some minor roads take you south for a very brief stint on the A66 to Troutbeck before you reach the Old Coach Road. This seven-kilometre track is a treat – the surface is often challenging but the views are something else. The exact age of the road is unclear, but people have been using it to move livestock for hundreds of years. A fun descent on the Old Coach Road takes you down towards Threlkeld, before a blissfully easy stint on the Keswick Railway Path returns you to Keswick for a thoroughly deserved brew!

One of the hallmarks of this ride is its remoteness; make sure you take enough supplies with you. Take this route and chip away at it; take as little or as much time as you need. I guarantee it will be worth it!

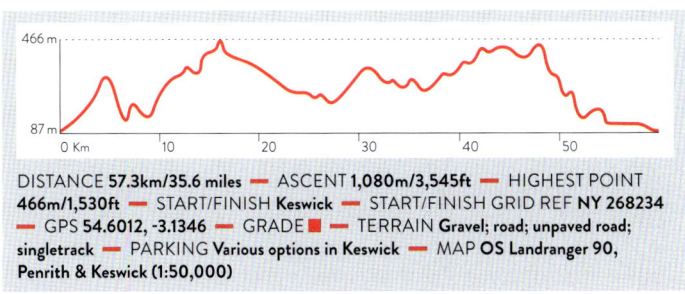

DISTANCE **57.3km/35.6 miles** — ASCENT **1,080m/3,545ft** — HIGHEST POINT **466m/1,530ft** — START/FINISH **Keswick** — START/FINISH GRID REF **NY 268234** — GPS **54.6012, -3.1346** — GRADE ■ — TERRAIN **Gravel; road; unpaved road; singletrack** — PARKING **Various options in Keswick** — MAP **OS Landranger 90, Penrith & Keswick (1:50,000)**

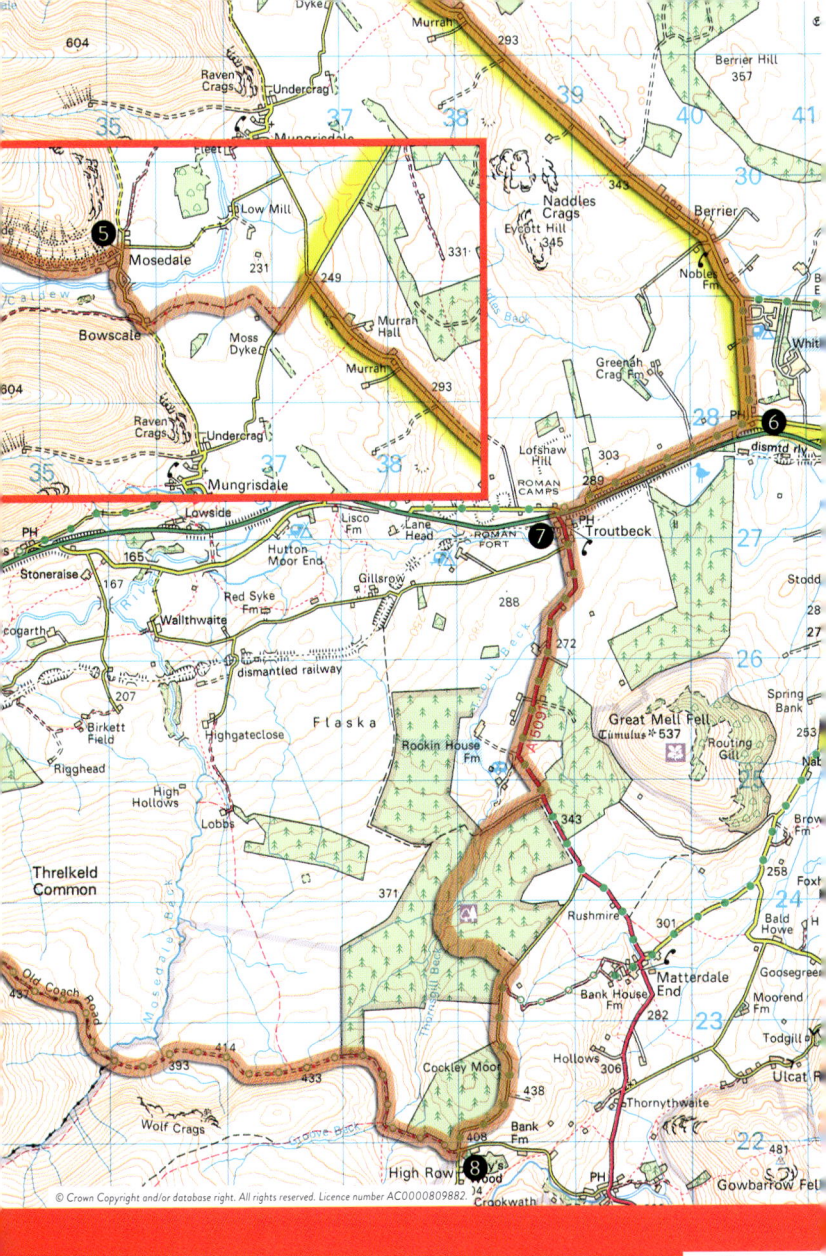

14 SKIDDAW HOUSE & THE OLD COACH ROAD

85

Directions

S Head north out of Keswick, crossing the River Greta on Station Road. Where the road curves to the right, go **SA** on to a cycle path (NCN route 71). Continue **SA** through a car park to reach a mini roundabout; turn **L** on to Brundholme Road. Shortly afterwards turn **R**, following the signpost for *Windebrowe* and *Brundholme*. Cross a bridge over the A66 then immediately afterwards turn **L** on to a gravel track contouring around the side of Latrigg. Keep **R** after 700m then continue for 500m to reach a junction with the Cumbria Way.

2 Turn **R** on to the Cumbria Way. On the northern side of Latrigg turn **R** through a gate to meet a parking area at the roadhead. Continue **SA** through a gate at the head of the parking area towards Brundholme. After descending, turn **L** adjacent to the end of a minor road and follow this rough track around before climbing to the farm buildings at Wescoe. Turn **R** and follow this lane towards Threlkeld.

1 COMING ROUND THE VALLEY. © JOHN COEFIELD. 2 VIEWS OF HALL'S FELL RIDGE AND SHARP EDGE ON BLENCATHRA. © JOHN COEFIELD. 3 RIVER GRETA. 4 OVER THE BECK. © JOHN COEFIELD.

❸ After about 1km, you'll meet the road into Threlkeld – turn **L** and ride into the village. Turn **L** at the junction signed *Blease Road Leading to Blencathra* and follow this as it climbs (sometimes steeply) above the village. Keep **R** by the entrance to Blencathra Field Centre and follow the public bridleway which becomes a gravel track. This heads north into the depths and fold of the valley, above and following the Glenderaterra Beck; there are some nice undulating sections here and a couple of beck crossings to negotiate. Cross a bridge and climb to reach a path junction with the Cumbria Way. Turn **R** along the Cumbria Way for a tricky climb to Skiddaw House.

❹ Turn **R** at Skiddaw House, heading north-east on singletrack and still following the Cumbria Way. Continue on a rough track alongside the River Caldew for 5.5km to reach a footbridge. (There is the option here to extend the route to a small bothy if you want an overnight stop. The Great Lingy Hut is 2.3km to the north-west; grid reference: NY 311335.) Cross the bridge (the surface becomes tarmac here) and keep **SA**, heading east along the River Caldew, leaving the Cumbria Way. Enjoy the steady descent for 3km to reach a junction in Mosedale.

■ **14 SKIDDAW HOUSE & THE OLD COACH ROAD**

5 Turn **R** on to the road, cross a bridge then pass a few houses in Bowscale. Just after the houses, turn **L** on to a gravel track. Follow this for 1.4km to reach a road. Turn **L** on to the road (you're now on NCN route 71). Turn **R** at the next junction (staying with NCN route 71 and following the signpost for *Berrier* and *Greystoke*). Continue for just over 5km (passing the beautiful Eycott Hill Nature Reserve on the right) to reach a junction opposite the Sportsman's Inn.

6 Turn **R** on to the road. After 1.5km turn **R** on to the cycle trail which runs alongside the A66, heading west. Cross the A66 at the traffic island and keep heading west on the cycle trail on the other side of the A66. Shortly afterwards, turn **L** on to the A5091 (staying with NCN route 71; signposted *Troutbeck*) to reach Troutbeck village.

7 Follow the A5091 heading south for 2.5km (passing Great Mell Fell on your left) then turn **R** on to a gravel track at the back of a lay-by with a *Forestry Commission: Matterdale* sign). Follow the track for 1.2km, keeping **L** at any junctions to reach a minor road. Turn **R** on to the road and continue for 2km to reach a junction and parking area near High Row.

Coffee and food
Fellpack, Lake Road Brunch, The Square Orange or Cafe West, Keswick.

Bike shops
Biketreks, Keswick.

5 SINGLETRACK ALONG THE CUMBRIA WAY. © JOHN COEFIELD. **6** VIEWS FROM SKIDDAW HOUSE. © JOHN COEFIELD. **7** KESWICK RAILWAY PATH. **8** NO STARING! © JOHN COEFIELD.

8 Turn **R** on to the Old Coach Road (signposted *St John's in the Vale; Unsuitable for motor vehicles*). Stay with this unsealed and unclassified county road for the next 7km. It's rough – very rough – along with some steep drops in places, so care is needed. The road undulates around the side of Matterdale Common passing Wolf Crags – popular with climbers and paragliders – on your left; the views really open up here. There is a little drop down to Mariel Bridge then a stiff climb up to the highest point of the road underneath Clough Head, before a teeth-rattling descent towards Threlkeld.

9 Turn **R** underneath Threlkeld Knotts, leaving the Old Coach Road and heading north. At the gated entry to Threlkeld Quarry, keep **R** on to a moorland path and skirt the quarry keeping the wall to your left. Bear around and downhill to the left and pass through a gate on to a lane by the buildings at Newsham. Descend to the A66, carefully cross the road and ride up the road almost opposite into Threlkeld village. Follow the road westwards all the way through the village until you rejoin the A66; use the cycleway by the road to pick up the Keswick Railway Path at its eastern end by the road bridge over the River Greta. Follow the path for a well-deserved, easy final stretch back into Keswick, turning **L** at the end of the trail to return to your starting point.

■ 14 **SKIDDAW HOUSE & THE OLD COACH ROAD**

VIEWS FROM LOUGHRIGG FELL OVER TO WETHERLAM.

15 **LAKELAND 270**
270km/170 miles

Introduction

When I was writing this guidebook, I wanted to create the ultimate Lake District gravel route – something to truly showcase the variety of this stunning national park, from the rolling hills and quaint hamlets in the south-east to the tallest mountains in England over in the north-west. Think of it as gravel's version of the Lakeland 200.

This route is built up of sections I've ridden over the years; I've tried to make it as gravel friendly as possible – easier said than done in the Lakes! Mainly comprised of bridleways, byways and minor roads, this route takes you off the beaten track and skirts round the busiest honeypots, but is never too far from the next hamlet or village. I developed this route with the warmer seasons in mind – you could break it down into three big days, five moderate days or, if you wanted to make it very leisurely, over a week. Taken slowly, it is achievable for all. My ideal scenario is to do this route over a week – take as much time as you can, you'll have a much better time when you're not up against the clock.

Having said all that, do not underestimate this ride; in parts it can be particularly slow going. It's been pieced together in the best possible way to give you as much riding as possible. In wetter weather and in the winter, bridleways through fields will become particularly boggy; in some cases they may be flooded. I encourage you to take a good look at the route and bear in mind the current conditions before setting off.

I've also suggested some local and independent businesses I've stayed with or visited over the years that I'd highly

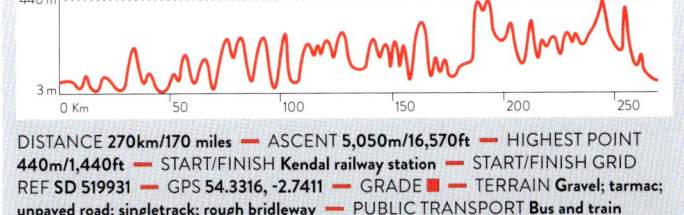

DISTANCE **270km/170 miles** — ASCENT **5,050m/16,570ft** — HIGHEST POINT **440m/1,440ft** — START/FINISH **Kendal railway station** — START/FINISH GRID REF **SD 519931** — GPS **54.3316, -2.7411** — GRADE ■ — TERRAIN **Gravel; tarmac; unpaved road; singletrack; rough bridleway** — PUBLIC TRANSPORT **Bus and train connections to Kendal** — PARKING **Various options in Kendal** — MAP **OS Landranger 89, West Cumbria; 90, Penrith & Keswick; 91, Appleby-in-Westmorland; 96, Barrow-in-Furness & South Lakeland; 97, Kendal & Morecambe (1:50,000)**

recommend; some of these are a little off route, but I find that a comfy bed and a good breakfast are worth travelling a little extra distance for. There are many other options but I've stayed within the remit of my own personal experiences. Work out how long you think it'll take you to do the route, and look for accommodation to suit your own itinerary. Camping or wild camping, when done responsibly and with the landowner's permission, is another option if you want to turn this route into a bikepacking adventure. Further information about camping and wild camping in the national park can be found at *www.lakedistrict.gov.uk/visiting/where-to-stay/wild-camping*

I think that the toughest part of the route is from kilometres 50 to 100, particularly the part between Coniston and Eskdale. Also, the further west you get the more remote this ride becomes, so being self-sufficient is an absolute must. Many, but certainly not all, of the small villages have a shop, but you can't always rely on it being open.

Arriving back in Kendal having finished the route you may have to pinch yourself – I do believe this is the best way to see the Lake District National Park in all of its glory. This really is quite a journey and it will provide plenty of stories to share. Pick a good weather window and just enjoy seeing the Lakes by bike.

1 NO SHORTAGE OF CLIMBING HERE. **2** LAYERS OF THE SOUTH LAKELAND FELLS. **3** STILL MORNING AT BLEA TARN. **4** VIEW FROM MISLET BROW.

Directions

Overview directions only. If you intend to take on this route, download the GPX file (page vii) to help with your planning and navigation.

S Start out from Kendal and make your way along the minor roads and bridleways of the South Lakes. I ride frequently here; it is largely overlooked by tourists, so traffic and human activity are minimal. Roll through the lowlands of the Lyth Valley towards Witherslack before making your way round various minor roads, bridleways and fire roads to meet the bottom of Windermere at Newby Bridge.

2 As you skirt round the bottom of Windermere and start heading further west the landscape really changes. Just before getting into Greenodd you pass over the estuary where the River Leven and Rusland Pool meet to drain into Morecambe Bay. I recommend stopping in Greenodd so you can visit Bakehouse Born and Bread – it is sensational and will give you some much-needed extra energy as from here you will have to start digging a little deeper as the going gets tougher. I think

■ 15 LAKELAND 270

this section is the hardest mainly due to the terrain and undulation of the route. Head round Bethecar Moor (the views open up to the north here and you'll be able to see right down Coniston Water) to reach Blawith.

❸ From Blawith there are some road miles over to the plantation at Broughton Moor, west of Coniston Water. I really like the ride through here – there's an interesting old settlement as you come alongside Appletree Worth Beck. Head out of the plantation and descend into Stephenson Ground then take a minor road south towards Carter Ground, skirting the south-east flank of Raven's Crag. Traverse the Dunnerdale Fells then cross the River Duddon to reach Ulpha. A stint on a minor road over Ulpha Fell and Birker Fell takes you down to Eskdale and the village of Eskdale Green.

❹ Restock and refuel here (as it's a while before the next opportunity), before joining the bridleways and fire roads of Miterdale Forest. Be ready for the steep descent off the top of Irton Fell where you can see Latterbarrow to the west and Wast Water with Scafell Pike behind it to the east. Cross the River Irt to reach Nether Wasdale. (A detour to have a closer look at Wast Water is worth doing – take a dip and admire The Screes of Illgill Head.)

❺ The next section finds you working your way through lowlands, coppices and plantation forests. Minor roads and a bridleway take you to Blengdale Forest and on through Scalderskew Wood. Cross Worm Gill then climb up the side of Town Bank on Kinniside Common. A short section on minor roads takes you to the fire roads of Lowther Park, before another short section of road takes you to Ennerdale Bridge at the western end of Ennerdale Water, a lovely quiet part of the Lakes.

❻ Follow the bridleway along the shore of Ennerdale Water then turn north and pick up NCN route 71. Pass through Lamplugh then, leaving NCN route 71 behind for now, follow a series of bridleways near the western shore of Loweswater. Head north then east over Whin Fell and into Low Lorton on possibly one of the best sections of 'gravel' in the entire route in terms of the surface underneath your tyres. I would describe it as traffic-free doubletrack – it is straight and smooth so you can switch off and just enjoy the ride.

❼ From Low Lorton, join NCN route 71 again to head back towards civilisation as you meander around Whinlatter Forest Park and descend to Braithwaite. The busyness of Keswick might be a bit of a shock after the quiet of the Western Lakes, but it is a good place to stop and enjoy some local cafes, have a swim in Derwent Water and visit the pencil museum. Also, make sure you are well stocked up for the next part of the ride, as there aren't many shops or cafes.

5 STRIDING EDGE FROM HELVELLYN. 6 VIEW FROM BROUGHTON MOOR.

Food and accommodation
The Farmer's Arms, Lowick Green; Bower House Inn, Eskdale; YHA Borrowdale; YHA Keswick; Pooley Bridge Inn or the Crown Inn, Pooley Bridge.

Bike shops
Brucie's Bike Shop or Giant, Kendal; Biketreks, Ings, Grizedale or Keswick.

❽ Heading east now, join the Keswick Railway Path to Threlkeld (see routes 05, 07 and 14), go south to St John's in the Vale then go east on the Old Coach Road (see route 14). Skirt around the northern end of Ullswater to reach Pooley Bridge.

❾ Continue east to Askham (see route 06). You'll observe the change in landscape here as you emerge from the mountains – the limestone moorland and rolling hills are reminiscent of the nearby Yorkshire Dales. Heading south now, you skirt between the most eastern Cumbria fells and the Howgills along some interesting minor roads and bridleways to reach Shap. The next part of the route is quite isolated, so stock up well.

❿ Continue to head south on bridleways and minor roads, passing between the M6 and Wet Sleddale Reservoir. A short stint on the A6 takes you to the delightful trail through the 'other' Borrowdale and over Whinfell Beacon (see route 13), before quiet lanes and bridleways take you back to Kendal.

APPENDIX

Tourist information centres
www.lakedistrict.gov.uk
www.visitlakedistrict.com

Bowness-on-Windermere	**T** 01539 724 555
Keswick	**T** 01539 724 555
Ullswater	**T** 01539 724 555

Weather
www.metoffice.gov.uk
www.mwis.org.uk

Bike shops

Arragon's Cycles, Penrith	**T** 01768 890 344
Biketreks, Keswick, Grizedale Forest and Ings	**T** 01539 431 245
Brucie's Bike Shop, Kendal	**T** 01539 727 230
Cyclewise, Cockermouth	**T** 01900 821 998
Cyclewise, Whinlatter	**T** 01768 778 711
Ghyllside Cycles, Ambleside	**T** 01539 433 592
Giant, Kendal	**T** 01539 728 057
Leisure Lakes Bikes, Ulverston	**T** 01229 581 116
Push Cartel, Ambleside	**T** 01539 431 408
Wheelbase, Staveley	**T** 01539 821 443
4Play Cycles, Cockermouth	**T** 01900 823 377

Bike hire

Biketreks, Grizedale Forest	**T** 01539 431 245
Country Lanes, Windermere	**T** 01539 444 544
Cyclewise, Whinlatter	**T** 01768 778 711
Ghyllside Cycles, Ambleside	**T** 01539 433 592
Lake District Bikes, Lowick Green	**T** 07887 731 552
Total Adventure Bike Hire, Windermere	**T** 01539 443 151
Windermere Canoe Kayak, Windermere	**T** 01539 444 451

Vertebrate Publishing
At Vertebrate Publishing we publish books to inspire adventure.

It's our rule that the only books we publish are those that we'd want to read or use ourselves. We endeavour to bring you beautiful books that stand the test of time and that you'll be proud to have on your bookshelf for years to come.

The Peak District was the inspiration behind our first books. Our offices are situated on its doorstep, minutes away from world-class climbing, biking and hillwalking. We're driven by our own passion for the outdoors, for exploration, and for the natural world; it's this passion that we want to share with our readers. We aim to inspire everyone to get out there. We want to connect readers – young and old – with the outdoors and the positive impact it can have on well-being. We think it's particularly important that young people get outside and explore the natural world, something we support through our publishing programme.

As well as publishing award-winning new books, we're working to make available many out-of-print classics in both print and digital formats. These are stories that we believe are unique and significant; we want to make sure that they continue to be shared and enjoyed.

www.adventurebooks.com

About the author

Andrew Barlow grew up in a Cheshire farming family, so the outdoor lifestyle was distilled within him from a very young age. Now Andrew is a freelance storyteller within the outdoor industry and is an advocate for inclusive cycling. He started enjoying hiking and landscape photography while living in Manchester, often escaping the stresses of his corporate printing job to enjoy the golden triangle of national parks nearby – the Peak District, Lake District and Eryri (Snowdonia).

Andrew relocated to Cumbria in 2018 after quitting the rat race to slow down and enjoy his photography. He then rekindled his love for cycling by using his bike as a tool to explore the lanes, bridleways and cycle routes of Cumbria, rather than to commute to work within the city. This led to his first book – *Gravel Rides Lake District* – which was written with an inclusive ethos in mind, so everyone can enjoy cycling as much as he does.

@andrewbarlowphoto

Vertebrate Publishing
The UK's number one publisher of cycling guidebooks

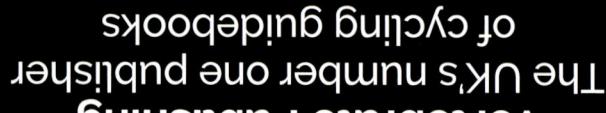

Available from bookshops or direct
Sign up to our newsletter to save 25%

www.adventurebooks.com

VP inspiring adventure

Food and drink

Cafes

Askham Stores, Askham	**T** 01931 712 187
Cafe Ambio, Grizedale Forest visitor centre	**T** 01229 860 496
Cafe West, Keswick	**T** 01768 775 947
Chesters by the River, Skelwith Bridge	**T** 01539 434 711
Copper Pot, Ambleside	
Fellpack, Keswick	**T** 01768 774 999
Fold Coffee, Kendal	**T** 07595 346 338
Granny Dowbekin's, Pooley Bridge	**T** 01768 486 453
Homeground, Windermere	**T** 01539 444 863
Joey's, Wray Castle	
Lake Road Brunch, Keswick	**T** 01768 785 474
Lanty Slee's, Great Langdale	
Lowther Castle Cafe, Askham	**T** 01931 712 192
Marra, Kendal	**T** 07557 958 497
More?, Staveley	**T** 01539 825 110
Mr Duffins Coffee, Staveley	**T** 01539 822 192
Podda & Wren, Kendal	**T** 01539 272 144
The Apple Pie, Ambleside	**T** 01539 433 679
The Bakery at No.4, Kendal	**T** 07500 772 134
The Green Housekeeper, Coniston	**T** 01539 441 925
The Lingholm Kitchen, Lingholm Estate	**T** 01768 771 206
Threlkeld Coffee Shop, Threlkeld	**T** 01768 779 501
Undercrag Cafe, Torver	**T** 07768 738 849
Wilf's Cafe, Staveley	**T** 01539 822 329

Pubs

Bower House Inn, Eskdale	**T** 01946 723 244
Britannia Inn, Elterwater	**T** 01539 437 210
Crown Inn, Pooley Bridge	**T** 01768 425 869
Drunken Duck Inn, Barngates	**T** 01539 436 347
Kittchen, Hawkshead	**T** 01539 436 920
Pooley Bridge Inn, Pooley Bridge	**T** 01768 486 215
The Farmer's Arms, Lowick Green	**T** 01229 481 160
The Square Orange, Keswick	**T** 01768 773 888
Three Shires Inn, Little Langdale	**T** 01539 437 215

Accommodation
Hostels
The YHA has hostels across the national park, including in Keswick and at Coniston Coppermines. Along with dorm rooms, many have private rooms, camping pitches, Landpods or yurts.
www.yha.org.uk

Derwentwater Independent Hostel .... **T** 01768 777 246
Elterwater Hostel .... **T** 01539 437 245
Kendal Hostel .... **T** 01539 724 066
www.independenthostels.co.uk

Hotels, self-catering and B&B
www.lakedistrict.gov.uk
www.visitlakedistrict.com

Camping
www.campsites.co.uk
www.ukcampsite.co.uk

Public transport
www.lakedistrictonboard.com/transport/lake-district-buses/
@windermereferry

Other publications
Great British Gravel Rides
Markus Stitz, Vertebrate Publishing   *www.adventurebooks.com*

Gravel Rides Scotland
Ed Shoote, Vertebrate Publishing   *www.adventurebooks.com*

Lake District Mountain Biking
Richard Staton and Chris Gore, Vertebrate Publishing   *www.adventurebooks.com*

Bikepacking England
Emma Kingston, Vertebrate Publishing   *www.adventurebooks.com*

Pennine Bridleway
Hannah Collingridge, Vertebrate Publishing   *www.adventurebooks.com*